بسم الله الرحمن الرحيم

LOVE FOR ALLAH

And those who strive in Us -

We will certainly guide them to Our paths...

(Surah Al 'Ankabūt, Verse Sixty-Nine)

LOVE FOR ALLAH

FAQĪR ZULFIQAR AHMAD *NAQSHBANDI*

الله عزّ وجلّ

FAQIR PUBLICATIONS
Chicago

Second Edition
Printed in the United States of America
ISBN: 0-9712761-0-2

Published by:
FAQIR PUBLICATIONS™
PO Box 597104
Chicago, IL 60659-7104
www.faqirpublications.com
info@faqirpublications.com

CONTENTS

TRANSLATOR'S FOREWORD

All praise is due to Allah ﷻ, lord of the Universe and may peace and blessings be upon Muhammad ﷺ, His beloved Messenger. Allah ﷻ states in His Glorious Book:

و الذين ءامنوا أشد حبا لله

And those who believe have intense love for Allah. (2:165)

Allah ﷻ describes an attribute of the believers thus: they are extreme in their love for Him. In fact, they are mad in their love for Him. With the construct "*those who believe*," Allah ﷻ challenges the believers by describing a characteristic of true belief. It is as if His verse calls out, "O ye who claim to believe, who profess that the light [*nūr*] of faith is in your hearts, know that the true believers are intense in their love for Allah."

A famous commentator of the Quran once said, "I can summarize the commentary [*tafsīr*] of the entire Quran in a single sentence: gain the pleasure of Allah ﷻ through worship, gain the pleasure of Allah's Messenger ﷺ through following [*ittibā'a*] his *sunnah*, and gain the pleasure of creation through serving them."

Perhaps the greatest challenge facing Muslims today is the force of secularism, whose root aim is to sever man from the sacred, and to distance a believer from his Lord. As a result of these forces, religion is reduced to activism and empty slogans.

The heart is always in love with someone. Either love for Allah ﷾ permeates the heart or love for other than Allah ﷾ will permeate it. Nowadays, love of the material world [*dunyā*] has overpowered our hearts and through heedlessness we have become increasingly distant from our Lord. Truly, love for Allah ﷾ is the need of the times. Our problem is two-fold: first, we are unaware of our Lord and ignorant of the close relationship he wishes to have with us. Allah ﷾ states, "*Verily, I am near.*" [2:186] And second, we lack any desire to be close to our Creator.

In all times there are pious ones who emerge to renew the faith in people's hearts and draw them closer to Allah ﷾. The author of this volume, *Shaykh* Zulfiqar Ahmad, is one such person. By writing this book, the author reminds us of that which we have forgotten: love for Allah ﷾. Indeed, he instills within us a desire to attain proximity with Allah ﷾. Anyone who reads this work with an open heart will find himself newly aware of his Lord and will find the flame of love lit in his heart. The love of Allah ﷾ that permeates the heart of the author is indelibly transferred to the heart of the reader.

By the grace of Allah ﷾ this is the first English edition of one of *Shaykh* Zulfiqar Ahmad's books. We have made a sincere effort to render all terms into English. Where we felt the need to preserve Arabic terminology, a translation of the term follows in brackets. On occasion, the editor has inserted subchapter headings and explanatory footnotes to ensure clarity and smooth transitions. Throughout the text, the Glorious Quran is cited by referencing the chapter number first followed by the verse. Any errors or mistranslations are our own, for which we seek Allah's سبحانه وتعالى forgiveness and the reader's pardon.

Many people have taken part in the preparation of this book. Preliminary drafts were first prepared by Mufti A.H. Elias and Brigadier Ashfaq Ashraf, which formed the basis for the present edition prepared by Kamaluddin and Sobia Ahmed. May Allah سبحانه وتعالى reward all those who participated in this project.

I humbly request that each reader sincerely pray for all those whose tireless efforts helped produce this unique work.

May Allah سبحانه وتعالى burn the flame of love in all of our hearts and guide us on the path of remembrance and reflection leading to His proximity.

Kamaluddin Ahmed

Rabi' Al-Thani 1422 | July 2001

PROLOGUE

While on a religious tour of South Africa, this humble writer wanted to reply to a friend's letter. As his letter was written with truly loving words, the thought arose in my heart: if a seeker [*murīd*] can send his *shaykh* such a loving tribute, then this *faqīr*[1] too should write something for his True Beloved ﷾ concerning Love for Allah [*'Ishq Ilāhī*]. Once my pen was placed on paper, an endless stream of thoughts began to flow. On one hand, there were numerous gatherings to attend and many people to meet, and on the other hand, a lack of time and the rigors of travel. Yet, this *faqīr* would daily yield bits and pieces of his thoughts to paper. Sometimes due to my own lack of knowledge, the thought would arise:

> ***How can this beauty be compressed into the structure of words?***
> ***I fear that Your perfection be not insulted.***

---

[1] *Faqīr* literally means, "needy one." Here it refers to that person who has acknowledged his complete dependence, and therefore need, upon Allah ﷾.

However, the importance of the topic did not allow me to back away. The truth is:

> *For the mind, heart, and sight, the first* shaykh *is* 'ishq [*love*].
> *If there be not* 'ishq, *then* sharī'ah [*Islamic law*] *and* dīn [*religion*]
> *become but idols of whimsical ideas.*

Today people have become so arrested by the love of the material world [*dunyā*] that they are always occupied in obtaining its goods. Outwardly they speak of love for Allah ﷻ to console their hearts. However, the truth of the matter is that in the Court of the King of Love ﷻ, there is no such thing as division of the heart. There, one must step with concentration and deliberation and must close the eyes of one's heart to everything but Allah ﷻ. How unfortunate that we are not even willing to take the first step of closing our physical eyes.

In this book, this *faqīr* let his pen flow freely, writing all that came to mind. If religious scholars find any shortcomings, please bring them to the attention of the publishers, and may your reward be with Allah ﷻ. Finally, the readers are requested for their heartfelt *du'at* [supplications].

Faqīr Zulfiqar Ahmad *Naqshbandi Mujaddidī*

1

THE IMPORTANCE OF LOVE FOR ALLAH

All praise is due to Allah ﷻ,[1] who deemed man worthy to be the foremost of His creation. Allah ﷻ states:

لقد خلقنا الإنسان في أحسن تقويم

We indeed created humanity in the best of forms. (95:4)

Allah ﷻ, the Lord of the universe, plants the seed of His love in the heart of every human at the time of their birth. This is why every person is born in the original state [*fitrah*] of Islam. A hadith states:

كل مولود يولد على فطرة الإسلام

Every baby is born on the fitrah *of Islam.*

It is this *fitrah*, rather than rational arguments, that compels every person to believe in the existence of Allah ﷻ and to worship Him alone.

---

[1] ﷻ literally means, "Glorious and Exalted is He" and is mentioned after the name of Allah ﷻ.

Life is given in order to worship,
Life without worship is shameful.

If the inherent love for Allah سبحانه و تعالى was removed from humanity, nothing but bestiality would remain. Truly, nothing of worth exists in the temporary life of this world [*dunyā*] other than love for Allah سبحانه و تعالى.

Only when love for Allah سبحانه و تعالى flourishes in the heart and captivates the eyes does life itself become wondrous.

The way of love is unlike all other ways,
The creed of lovers is distinct from all other creeds.

Honor and disgrace in life are dependent upon love for Allah سبحانه و تعالى. Allah سبحانه و تعالى honors His servants with the verse:

و لقد كرمنا بني آدم

We have indeed honored mankind (17:70)

and Allah سبحانه و تعالى adorns man with the verse:

و فضلناهم على كثير

And We have preferred them over many others (17:70)

Allah سبحانه و تعالى bestows honor and respect upon humanity due to its love for Him.

He who is the lover of the beauty of Allah
Is the leader of all of creation.

The crux of the beginning and end of life, its origin and destination, is love for Allah سبحانه و تعالى.

Love is the beginning; love is the end; love is everything,
Love is the branch; love is the tree; love is the flower.

Instead of sustaining and nourishing, infertile land causes a seed to erode and wither away. Similarly, rather than fostering love for Allah, an environment saturated in sin engulfs and stifles the heart in heedlessness and neglect. In a nurturing environment, the seed of Allah's love flourishes and blooms giving off a beautiful fragrance. In every virtuous environment, you will find that the awareness of Allah is the focus of people's lives.

One knows not the color and scent of this pleasant flower,
That attracts every bird in the garden toward it.

So what if the enamored one is insane in the love of Allah?
Look and you shall find the whole world His admirer.

Truly, the degree to which Allah has been sought; the zeal with which He has been loved; the extent to which He has been remembered; the yearning with which He has been invoked; the amount that He has been worshipped; and the fervor with which He has been admired and adored stands far above all else. No other entity in the universe bears comparison. All of creation loves Allah.

PRINCIPLES PERTAINING TO LOVE FOR ALLAH

The First Principle

The human body is composed of limbs and organs, each with a unique trait: seeing is the trait of the eye; listening is the trait of the ear; and smelling is the trait of the nose. Similarly, loving is the trait of the heart; the heart is always in love with someone.

Be it with a stone, God, or anyone else,
There comes not tranquility without loving.

The heart is the ocean of love; love is its act,
Guard it a thousand ways; it will still fall in love.

The Second Principle

A person usually falls in love for two reasons. The first is when the beloved's essential being [*dhāt*] and attributes [*sifāt*] are distinct and superior to all others. Such is Allah ﷻ, who is perfect in every way and beyond any comparison. How beautiful and magnificent must the Creator of all the world's beauty be! It is only natural that a person is attracted to his Lord.

The second reason is when the beloved has authority and is involved in every aspect of one's life. Such is Allah ﷻ, who at any moment can relieve one's grief or sorrow. This is the reason why everyone instinctively turns to Allah ﷻ in times of distress.

At every instance of grief, comfort was found in Thee,
At every turn, bewildered, I took Thy name.

The Third Principle

There is such sweetness and pleasure in the name of Allah ﷻ that by repeatedly invoking His name every sorrow is turned into joy.

He who is distressed turns his attention in that direction,
Certainly there must be something in the name of Allah.

The Fourth Principle

A person should remain unaffected by the ever-changing conditions of life and remember Allah ﷻ at every moment.

Although trapped daily to earn a livelihood,
Never did I neglect thinking of You.

The Fifth Principle

The heart that is not imprinted with love for Allah ﷻ finds no pleasure in living. Whatever one's state, never should the court of the True Beloved ﷻ be abandoned.

The Sixth Principle

The person whose heart experiences the sweetness of love for Allah ﷻ attains focus and tranquility in life.

Seeking neither means nor objects, my needs I myself fulfill,
By thanking You, thinking of You, and taking Your name.

The Seventh Principle

No veils remain on the perception of what exists between the Throne [*'Arsh*] of Allah ﷻ and the ground for he whose eyes are adorned with the antimony [*kuhl*] of the love of Allah ﷻ. When the one who loves Allah ﷻ [*'āshiq*] gazes introspectively, he perceives himself full of sin and defects. And when he directs his gaze upon the Beloved ﷻ, he finds Him to be the endower and bestower of all things. Consequently, he places all hope in Him and waits expectantly at His door.

إلهي كيف أدعوك و أنا عاص
و كيف لا أدعوك و أنت كريم

O Allah, how may I call unto You, when I am but a sinner,
Yet how may I not call unto You, when You are the Most Gracious?

The Eighth Principle

The *'āshiq* is never heedless of the True Beloved ﷻ; not even for a moment. He remains waiting in vigil, knowing not when the doors of his Beloved ﷻ might open.

> ***Be not heedless of the Lord for even the blink of an eye,***
> ***Lest He direct His attention toward you, and find you unaware.***

It is for this reason that the scholars of *tasawwuf*[2] have said:

من غمض عينه عن الله تعالى طرفة عين لم يصل إلى مقصوده

The person who diverts his attention from Allah for even the blink of an eye will not attain his goal.

The Ninth Principle

There is no place in the heart of an *'āshiq* for anyone other than his Beloved ﷻ. Although he is unable to see the True Beloved ﷻ with his physical eyes, he is able to perceive Him with the eyes of his heart.

حبيب ليس بعد له حبيب
و ما لسواه نصيب
حبيب غائب عن بصري و شخصي
و لكن عن فؤادي لا يغيب

> *My Beloved is such that there is no beloved besides Him,*
> *Nor is there place in my heart for any other.*
> *My Beloved may be hidden from my sight,*
> *But He is not absent from my heart.*

---

[2] *Tasawwuf* is the science of the purification of the heart and soul.

The Tenth Principle

The sole objective of a sincere *'āshiq* is to meet his Beloved ﷻ. He passes his entire life in anticipation of this meeting. His heart refuses to be attracted toward anything else.

أنت أنسي و همتي و سروري
قد أبى القلب أن يحب سواكا
يا عزيزي و همتي و مرادي
طال شوقي متى يكون لقاكا
ليس سؤالي من الجنان نعيم
غير أني أريد لقاكا

You are my dear, my motivation, my happiness,
My heart refuses to love any other besides You.
Oh my dear, my motivation, my desire,
Long have I been yearning, when will I finally meet You?
I seek not the comforts of Heaven, my desire is only to meet You.

The Eleventh Principle

An *'āshiq* always yearns to join his Beloved ﷻ. This is the sole thought occupying his mind.

You are the true innermost desire of my heart,
Love of You is the deepest thought in my mind.
Whenever I glance at the world around me,
I find that today there was naught but You,
And that tomorrow holds naught but You.

The Twelfth Principle

When an *'āshiq* looks around, he finds the heedless people of the world [*ghāfil al-dunyā*] trapped in their desires. To him the world seems like a cage.

The Thirteenth Principle

Love for Allah ﷻ removes everything except Allah ﷻ from the heart of the sincere *'āshiq*. Indeed, his heart has no place for anything other than Allah ﷻ.

The Fourteenth Principle

The heart of the *'āshiq* desires to sacrifice everything for the sake of his Beloved ﷻ.

> *May I forget everything in Your remembrance,*
> *And may I remember not anyone else.*
> *May I forsake unto Thee all dear to my heart,*
> *And may my heart be filled by You.*
> *May I set fire to my joys and happiness,*
> *And may my heart ache for Thee alone.*
> *May I be blinded to all I know,*
> *And may I turn only to Thee and none other.*

The Fifteenth Principle

In the material world [*dunya*], a person receives many things, while many other things remain out of reach. Whatever a person lacks, its substitute exists somewhere in the world. However, if someone is distant from Allah ﷻ, no substitute exists anywhere.

لكل شيئ إذا فارقته عوض
و ليس لله إن فارقت من عوض

> *For everything that you part from, there is a replacement,*
> *But if you disassociate from Allah, there is no replacement for Him.*

Hadrat[3] Abu Hurairah رضي الله عنه[4] reported that the blessed Prophet ﷺ[5] said that the best saying in the Arabic language is the poem of Labid:

---

[3] *Hadrat* literally means, "the venerable" and is used as a title of respect before the name of a religious figure.

ألا كل شيئ ما خلا الله باطل
و كل نعيم لا محالة ذائل

Verily, everything except Allah is false and spurious
And every blessing is undeniably fleeting and short-lived.

THE IMPORTANCE OF LOVE FOR ALLAH

Allah سبحانه وتعالى states in the Glorious Quran:

و الذين ءامنوا أشد حبا لله

And those who believe are intense in their love for Allah. (2:165)

The sign of complete and perfect faith [*imān*] is deep and intense love for Allah سبحانه وتعالى. This love remains constant over time, unaffected by the ever-changing conditions of life.

Love may be called love, but it is not love if it lacks intensity,
The ways of love are well established; there is no room for innovation.

Love for Allah سبحانه وتعالى changes the bitterness in a person's life to sweetness. No depression or anxiety afflicts the one who is attached to his Lord.

Love causes the bitter to become sweet, and silver to turn to gold,
Love erases all difficulty; love is the cure for all pain.

---

[4] رضي الله عنه literally means, "may Allah be pleased with him" and is mentioned after the name of a Companion of Prophet Muhammad ﷺ.

[5] ﷺ literally means, "may Allah bless him and grant him peace" and is mentioned after the name of Prophet Muhammad ﷺ.

THE DEFINITION OF LOVE
Hadrat Shibli (rah)[6] said:

سميت المحبة لأنها تمحو من القلب ما سوى المحبوب

Muhabbah [*love*] *is called* muhabbah *because it erases everything from the heart except the Beloved.*

The renowned master [*ustādh*] Abul Qasim Qushayri (rah) said:

المحبة محو المحب لصفاته و إثبات المحبوب بذاته

Muhabbah *is the erasure of the qualities* [sifāt] *of the lover, affirming the essential being* [dhāt] *of the Beloved.*

Hadrat Samnun Muhibb (rah) used to say:

ذهب المحبون لله بشرف الدنيا و الآخرة لأن النبي صلى الله عليه و سلم قال المرء مع من أحب

The lovers of Allah have taken the honor of this world and the honor of the Hereafter because the blessed Prophet ﷺ said: "A man will be with whom he loves."

Muhabbah is the name of a condition of the heart where the lover is restless to meet the Beloved ﷻ. When Allah ﷻ revealed the verse, in which He swears:

لعمرك

By your age (15:72),

---

[6] (rah) represents رحمة الله عليه which literally means, "may the mercy of Allah be upon him" and is mentioned after the name of a religious figure.

the blessed Prophet ﷺ stood so long in prayer that his feet became swollen. Allah ﷻ then revealed:

طه ما أنزلنا عليك القرآن لتشقى

Ta Ha. We did not send unto you [*O blessed Prophet*] *the Quran to cause you difficulty*. (20:1-2)

Imam Ghazali (rah) fell unconscious when he heard someone reciting the following couplet:

لقد لسعت حية الهوى كبدي
فلا طبيب لها و لا راقى
إلا الحبيب الذي شغف
فعنده رقيتي و ترياقي

The snake of love has stung my heart,
There is no doctor or charmer to cure it
Except the Beloved who fills my heart,
With Him lies my cure and charm.

A doctor was then called who, upon checking his pulse and examining his condition, declared that Imam Ghazali (rah) was suffering from the sickness of *muhabbah*.

TWO TRUE MAXIMS

In the realm of intense love [*'ishq*] and *muhabbah* two tenets are well established:

The First Maxim

No matter how much an *'āshiq* may praise the beauty and majesty of the True Beloved ﷻ, it always remains insufficient. Allah ﷻ states:

قل لو كان البحر مدادا لكلمت ربي لنفد البحر قبل أن تنفد كلمت ربي و لو
جئنا بمثله مددا

Say [O blessed Prophet]: Were the sea ink for the words of my Lord, verily the sea would be depleted before the Words of my Lord were exhausted, even if We brought the like thereof [another sea] to help. (18:109)

The Second Maxim

Allah ﷻ announces the name of the person who loves Him throughout the world. A hadith states that when a person draws near to Allah ﷻ through abundant worship [*'ibādāh*], then Allah ﷻ tells the Angel Jibril ﷺ[7] to take his name and announce it throughout the heavens and the Earth, "O people! Know that Allah loves so-and-so."

ثم يوضع له القبول في الأرض

Then acceptance is decreed for him on Earth.

He whose heart is alive with love does not die,
Rather his imprint lasts forever, recorded in the annals of history.

PROOFS OF ALLAH'S LOVE FOR HIS CREATION

A *hadīth qudsī*[8] relates:

كنت كنزا مخفيا فأحببت أن أعرف فخلقت الخلق

I (Allah) was a Hidden Treasure, then I wished to be discovered, therefore I created the universe.

---

[7] ﷺ literally means, "may peace be upon him" and is mentioned after the names of Angels and Prophets of Allah ﷻ.

[8] A *hadīth qudsī* is a narration in which Prophet Muhammad ﷺ relates a statement and attributes it directly to Allah ﷻ.

Thus, *'ishq*, *muhabbah*, and yearning were the motives behind the creation of the universe.

> *Love is the reason for the creation of the universe.*
> *Reflect upon the words of your Lord: 'I wished to be discovered.'*

The First Proof of Allah's Love for Creation

Allah ﷻ loves the believers and therefore states:

الله ولي الذين ءامنوا

Allah is the Friend of those who believe. (2:257)

It would have been suitable to say, "*Those who believe* are the friends of Allah," as it is *man* who befriends Allah ﷻ by professing the testimony of faith [*kalimah*] and becoming Muslim. Yet, Allah ﷻ revealed: "*Allah* is the Friend of those who believe," befriending the believers Himself. After being bestowed with the honor of Allah's ﷻ friendship, how can a person help but to sacrifice all for his Lord.

The Quran states that Allah ﷻ will create a nation such that:

يحبهم و يحبونه

Allah will love them and they will love Him. (5:54)

In this verse as well, Allah ﷻ first ascribes the attribute of loving to Himself, and then mentions the love of the believers.

The Second Proof of Allah's Love for Creation
Allah ﷻ states:

إن الله اشترى من المؤمنين أنفسهم و أموالهم بأن لهم الجنة

Indeed, Allah has purchased from the believers their souls and wealth in exchange for Heaven. (9:111)

A buyer's insistence on purchasing an item, despite his awareness of its defects, implies that the item is desirable irrespective of its faults. Allah ﷻ created humanity and is well aware of its faults and defects. He knows that man is weak [*daīf*] (4:28), hasty [*ajūlā*] (17:11), impatient [*halū'ā*] (70:19), stingy [*manū'ā*] (70:21), and irritable [*jazū'ā*] (70:20). Yet Allah ﷻ still chose to purchase him in exchange for Heaven. This is an indication that Allah ﷻ loves those who believe.

The Third Proof of Allah's Love for Creation
Hadrat Bayazid Bustami (rah) used to say:

المحبة استقلال الكثير من نفسك و استكثار القليل من حبيبك

Muhabbah *is to find trifling that which is given from oneself (to the Beloved), even though it is great; and to find great that which is received from one's Beloved, even if it is miniscule.*

Allah ﷻ bestows so many blessings on His servants that it is impossible to count them:

و إن تعدوا نعمت الله لا تحصوها

If you try to count the blessings of Allah, you will be unable to enumerate them. (14:34)

Nevertheless, despite these innumerable blessings, Allah ﷾ describes the material world as minimal:

قل متا ع الدنيا قليل

Say [*O blessed Prophet*], *the goods of the material world are but a trifle.* (4:77)

Allah ﷾ devalued His gift of unlimited blessings to a trifle. Yet when His servants remembered their Lord, Allah ﷾ described their limited remembrance [*dhikr*] as abundant:

و الذكرين الله كثير ا

...and those who remember Allah abundantly. (33:35)

This also is proof that Allah ﷾ has great love for the believers.

CONCLUSION

Allah's ﷾ love for the believers is mirrored in their hearts, causing them to overflow with His love.

و الذين ءامنو ا أشد حبا لله

And those who believe have intense love for Allah. (2:165)

2

THE EFFECTS OF LOVE FOR ALLAH

The blessings of love for Allah سبحانه وتعالى are enormous. When this love arises in a person's heart it leaves him illuminated from head to toe.

EFFECTS ON THE FACE

The face of a sincere *'āshiq* [one who loves Allah سبحانه وتعالى] glows with the spiritual radiance [*nūr*] of love for Allah سبحانه وتعالى. The knotted hearts of ordinary people become untied when they glance upon such a face. Once a group of Hindus accepted Islam and were asked why they did so. They pointed toward the face of *Allāmah* Anwar Shah Kashmiri (rah) and said, "This face can never be the face of a liar. Because he is Muslim, we also became Muslim."

Hadrat Ghulam Habib (rah), who later became known as "*Murshid al-'Ālam*",[9] was once in the sacred precincts of the Ka'bah, when his gaze fell upon the face of *Maulānā Qāri* Muhammad Tayyib (rah). *Hadrat Murshid al-'Ālam* (rah) greeted

---

[9] *Murshid al-'Ālam* literally means, "guide of the world." *Hadrat* Ghulam Habib (rah) was given this title due to his extensive travels throughout the world in the service of Islam.

him and asked, "How did you acquire such an illuminated face?" He smiled and replied, "I did not develop it myself; my spiritual guide [*shaykh*] produced it." Indeed, the mark of the people of Allah ﷻ [*ahlu'llāh*] has been mentioned in a hadith:

الذين إذا رؤوا ذكر الله

Those people who - when they are seen - Allah is remembered.

The faces of the *ahlu'llāh* are so bright with *nūr* that one remembers Allah ﷻ upon seeing them. Regarding the noble Companions [*Sahābah*] of the Prophet ﷺ, the Glorious Quran states:

سيماهم في وجوههم من أثر السجود

Their signs are on their faces, from the effects of prostrations. (48:29)

Once, when the blessed Prophet's ﷺ health had deteriorated considerably, he opened his door and looked into the *masjid* after *Hadrat* Abu Bakr ؓ had completed the prayer. The *Sahābah* ؓ narrate that at that moment the face of the blessed Prophet ﷺ was as though it was a page from the Quran.

While envisioning the scene in the Cave of Thawr when *Hadrat* Abu Bakr ؓ was looking upon the radiant face of the blessed Prophet ﷺ resting in his lap, *Hadrat* Shah Waliullah (rah) used to say: "O Abu Bakr! Your lap is like a desk and the radiant face of the blessed Prophet ﷺ like a manuscript of the Quran [*mushaf*]. O Abu Bakr! You are like the reciter who sits and reads the Quran."

Once *Hadrat* Abul-Hasan Kharqani (rah) stated that the face of Bayazid Bustami (rah) was so illuminated that anyone who saw him would have the knots (of disbelief) in his heart untied. A person objected, "When Abu Jahl saw the blessed Prophet ﷺ, the knot in his heart did not unravel. So how can you say that by looking at the face of Bayazid the knots in people's hearts were untied?" *Hadrat* Abul-Hasan Kharqani (rah) retorted, "O ignorant one, when did Abu Jahl ever look upon the radiant face of the blessed Prophet ﷺ?" The person was taken aback and asked incredulously, "How did he fail to look at the face of the blessed Prophet ﷺ?" *Hadrat* Kharqani (rah) then replied, "Abu Jahl looked at him as Muhammad bin Abdullah ﷺ. Had he even once viewed him as Muhammad the blessed Messenger ﷺ of Allah ﷻ, Abu Jahl would have never remained bereft of guidance."

Once Abdullah bin Salam ﵁, who had been a leading Jewish rabbi, came to the blessed Prophet ﷺ intending to ask him three questions. But upon looking at the *nūr* on the face of the blessed Prophet ﷺ, he accepted Islam. Someone asked him what caused him to divert from his original purpose in coming. He pointed toward the radiant face of the blessed Prophet ﷺ and said:

و الله هذا الوجه ليس وجه الكذاب

By Allah, this face is not the face of a liar.

When some of the rulers from the Successors[10] [*Tābi'īn*] sent a delegation to collect the *jizya*[11] from the disbelievers, the latter refused to pay. The officials asked, "Why do you refuse to pay us when you used to pay the *jizya* to our forefathers?" The disbelievers replied, "When your forefathers used to come, their clothes were old and torn, their hair was disheveled, and their eyes were streaked with red due to worshipping throughout the night. Yet their faces were so awe-inspiring that we were unable to raise our

---

[10] Successor is the title given to the generation of believers who came after the generation of the Companions [*Sahābah*] of the Prophet ﷺ.

[11] The *jizya* is a tax levied on non-Muslims living under Muslim rule.

eyes toward them. Your characteristics are not like theirs, nor will you be as just. Be gone, we will not give you anything."

EFFECTS ON THE GAZE

The gaze of a sincere *'āshiq* has such a powerful effect that wherever it falls, it leaves an impression. According to a poet:

> *A powerful effect indeed has the gaze of a friend of Allah,*
> *I saw it change the fate of thousands.*

Khwaja Ghulam Hasan Suwag (rah) was a *shaykh* of the Naqshbandi *ṭarīqah*[12] [spiritual path]. Whenever he looked attentively at a disbeliever, they would become Muslim. Many Hindu youth became Muslim in this manner. A number of Hindus filed a case accusing the *shaykh* of forcing their youth to become Muslim, and he was summoned to appear before the court. When he arrived, he asked why he had been summoned. The magistrate told him that he was accused of forcing Hindu youth to become Muslim. The *shaykh* was very surprised when he heard the nature of the charge levied against him. He turned his attention toward the group of Hindu plaintiffs and asked one of them, "Have I made you a Muslim?" In reply, the Hindu recited the testimony of faith [*kalimah*]. He then looked toward another, then a third, then a fourth – and each recited the *kalimah*. Fearing that the *shaykh* might also look toward him, the magistrate, who was a Hindu, said, "Enough. I now understand the situation." He dismissed the charges and the *shaykh* was exonerated with honor and respect.

Hadrat Shah Abdul Qadir (rah) spent eighteen years in spiritual retreat [*i'tikāf*] in a *masjid* in Delhi, India during which he translated the entire Quran. When he came out of the *masjid* his

---

[12] The Naqshbandi *ṭarīqah* is one of the four prominent methodologies [*madhhab*s] of spiritual development.

gaze fell upon a dog. It was so affected by the *nūr* of the *shaykh*'s gaze that afterwards, other dogs would trail behind it.

It is reported in a hadith:

العين حق

The effect of the evil and envious eye is a reality.

When some of the *Sahābah* ﷺ were affected by the evil eye, the blessed Prophet ﷺ taught them how to remove its influence. It is worth reflecting: if a gaze of envy, malice, and hatred can have ill effects, then why shouldn't the gaze of a sincere *'āshiq* – full of sincerity, mercy, and compassion - have an effect as well?

EFFECTS ON THE TONGUE

The tongue of a sincere *'āshiq* has such an effect that as soon as a supplication [*du'a*] to Allah ﷻ leaves his lips, it is accepted. And when he speaks, his words penetrate into the hearts of people. When an ordinary person says something it has no effect on others. When spoken by a person imbued with love for Allah ﷻ, the same words penetrate the innermost recesses of the heart.

Words which come from the heart
Have an indelible effect.

When the son of Shah Abdul Qadir Gangohi (rah) returned home after completing his religious studies, his father requested that he give some advice to a gathering of seekers [*sālikīn*]. His son delivered a talk replete with pearls of knowledge and his audience listened intently. Yet, they remained unmoved. At the end, his father addressed the gathering and said, "O *faqīrs*,[13] yesterday I left some milk out for my pre-dawn meal [*suhūr*] but a cat came and drank it." Upon hearing this, the *sālikīn* began to weep profusely. When they reached home after the gathering, *Hadrat* remarked, "Son, you gave an excellent talk yet not one iota reached their hearts. I merely mentioned a simple thing and it had a great effect." The son responded, "Dear father, only you can explain this." *Hadrat* explained, "When the heart is imbued with love for Allah ﷻ, then each word creates an impression on the hearts of the listeners."

EFFECTS ON SOIL

Understandably, intense love [*'ishq*] affects a person made of flesh and skin because he has a beating heart in his chest. However, *'ishq* is such that even when it meets the ground it renders the soil memorable. Why are the Taj Mahal and *Masjid* of Cordoba so famous and well known? Why are these buildings, which have been made from earth and soil, the highlight of history books? It is because *'ishq* was the motivation behind their construction.

---

[13] *Faqīr* literally means, "needy one." Here it refers to that person who has acknowledged his complete dependence, and therefore need, upon Allah ﷻ.

3

THE CONDITION OF THE LOVERS OF ALLAH IN THIS WORLD

Allah ﷻ states:

و تلك الأيام نداولها بين الناس

We keep alternating the days (good and bad) among mankind.
(3:140)

Like the tides of an ocean, the tides of life are perpetually changing. At times life is stormy; at other times life is calm. At times everything appears to blossom; at other times everything appears dismal. At times a person feels close to his Lord; at other times he feels distant. At times there is vitality; at other times there is listlessness. At times there is sickness; at other times there is health. Human conditions never remain the same. According to the poet *Allāmah* Iqbal:

> *Serenity is difficult in the workings of fate,*
> *Change is the only stable thing in time.*

The state of the one who loves Allah ﷻ [*'āshiq*] is affected by the changing conditions of life. Hence, at times he is happy and at other times he is sad. At times he feels close to his Creator and at other times he feels distant. At times there is affection and grace from the Beloved ﷻ and at other times there is anger and reproach. At times there is fervor and excitement and at other times there is peace and contentment. Whatever the circumstance, a sincere *'āshiq* always remains pleased with his Beloved ﷻ.

> *The Beloved's favors are regular, but His anger is occasional,*
> *My Beloved is to be lauded under all circumstances.*

Traversing the sea of love, an *'āshiq* experiences various states. These are briefly mentioned below.

Restlessness

The *'āshiq* is so anxious to reach [*wasl*] Allah ﷻ that he is unable to find rest, even for a moment. So occupied is he in the remembrance of his Beloved ﷻ.

> *I am not conscious of myself, nor of the world.*
> *I sit entranced by Your beauty,*
> *Ask the stars about the state of my life,*
> *I remain awake at night, in Your contemplation.*

Despair

When sadness and despair overcome an *'āshiq*, there is no outlet except for crying. This increases the beauty of one's love and wins over the seemingly distant Friend ﷻ.

Anticipation

The *'āshiq* desires that the Beloved ﷾ look at him with love. He anxiously awaits the mercy of the Creator of the universe. He knows that his aim would be fulfilled with a single glance from the Beloved ﷾.

> *Cast at least a slight glance toward the lovers,*
> *If not always, at least every now and then.*
> *With one glance, what hopes You plant in me,*
> *The hope for just one glance of You.*

Sacrifice

There can be no greater blessing than reaching [*wasl*] the Beloved ﷾. In comparison, everything else seems futile and trivial. For the realization of this *wasl*, the *'āshiq* is prepared to forego everything else.

> *Except for* wasl, *everything is useless,*
> *One* wasl *in exchange for one hundred worlds is graciously accepted.*
> *You ask me, 'What is entry into Heaven?'*
> *Meeting with the Friend is itself entry into Heaven.*

Development

Wherever Allah's ﷾ grace is directed, things begin to flourish. In contrast, (spiritual) withering away indicates Allah's ﷾ indifference.

> *What is this season of autumn? It is only His veiling,*
> *If He casts His gaze, it would soon be spring.*

Ecstasy

When the Beloved ﷾ showers His blessings, a sincere *'āshiq* cries. These are not tears of sorrow, but tears of joy. Both the happiness and sadness of love are expressed through tears. The heart of man is made of flesh, while the gaze of the Beloved ﷻ affects even stone.

A beautiful being glanced in my direction,
Now I can only sigh - speechless and bedazzled.
What fault is it of mine? My heart is but a piece of flesh,
His gaze would make a hole even in stone.

Separation

The heart of a sincere *'āshiq* is torn apart by separation and he can never find any solace in this condition.

O Beloved, my heart is mad about You,
Without worry, come into Your home, it is indeed Your home.
Sweeter You are to me than sugar and honey,
From Your separation, my heart is torn to pieces,
And these pieces were made for You.

Insignificance

Worldly objects do not attract the heart of the sincere *'āshiq*, nor does he give these things any importance. Compared with the pleasure of Allah ﷻ and of reaching Him, this decadent world has no significance.

Obsession

If anyone advises the sincere *'āshiq* that obsession is not appropriate he considers this person his enemy. In fact, he wishes that this person would catch just a glimpse of the beauty and splendor of the True Beloved ﷻ, so he too would become insane with love.

They ridicule my love for You.
O Beloved, cast a slight glance upon them too.
So they become like me, mad for You.

Measure

For a sincere *'āshiq*, his Beloved سبحانه وتعالى is the only criterion by which he gauges his friends and foes. If his own enemy were to fall in love with the Beloved سبحانه وتعالى, he would begin to regard him as a friend. If someone were to have no affection for his True Beloved سبحانه وتعالى, then he would regard him a foe.

Comfort

The *'āshiq* finds comfort in the remembrance of his Beloved سبحانه وتعالى. By taking His name again and again, his heart gains peace.

> *How much peace is attached to this name of Yours,*
> *Comfortable sleep can be found on a bed of thorns.*

Remembrance

An *'āshiq* cannot imagine one moment of his life devoid of the remembrance of his Beloved سبحانه وتعالى. His waking moments are full of thoughts of Him and his sleep is full of dreams of Him.

Thirst

Love for Allah سبحانه وتعالى is such that even if continuously sipped glass after glass, neither the thirst of the *'āshiq* would be quenched, nor the drink diminished.

> *I die when I think of You, then I come back to life,*
> *If the water of Your* wasl *did not exist, I would not be alive.*
> *Hope keeps me alive and desire kills me,*
> *For You, how many times have I lived, how many times have I died.*
> *I drink love, cup after cup,*
> *Yet the drink does not diminish, nor am I quenched.*

Eagerness

The name of the Beloved سبحانه وتعالى always remains in the heart of an *'āshiq* and the conception of Him always lingers before his eyes.

Thus, the heart and eyes of an *'āshiq* always remain eager for the Beloved ﷻ.

لي حبيب خياله نصب عيني
و اسمه ضمائري مكنون
إن تذكرته فكلي قلوب
و إن تأملته فكلي عيون

I have a Friend whose thoughts remain before my eyes,
And whose name is hidden in my heart.
When I remember Him, my entire body becomes my heart,
And when I look at Him, my entire body becomes my eyes.

Consolation

When a sincere *'āshiq* senses that his every sigh and lament is reaching his Beloved ﷻ, his heart gains consolation.

The heart of an 'āshiq finds contentment in the fact
That he has sent his sighs to the heavens.

Progression

An *'āshiq* advances toward his Lord with each tear. Just as distances in the physical world are crossed by foot, distances in the spiritual world are traversed by the shedding of tears.

Tearfulness

The condition of an *'āshiq* is truly worthy of pity. When there is separation, he cries craving for nearness [*wasl*]. And when there is *wasl*, he cries in profound gratitude. Perhaps intense love [*'ishq*] and crying go hand in hand.

To cry is the duty of the 'āshiq,
Without crying, there is no acceptance.
Whether the heart cries, or whether the eyes cry,
In love crying is necessary.
Some cry to see You, others cry at seeing You,
In profound love one must cry, whether in wasl *or in distance.*

Verbal Praise

When the eyes are in constant search of the Beloved ﷾ and the heart is flooded with His love, the tongue of the *'āshiq* remains engaged in singing His praise.

خيالك عيني و ذكرك في فمي
و مثواك في قلبي فأين تغيب

Your image is in my eyes, and Your remembrance on my lips,
Your abode is in my heart, so where can You hide?

Constant Reflection

When the sun rises, the *'āshiq* is reminded of his Beloved ﷾. When it sets, he is reminded of his Beloved ﷾. When an *'āshiq* sits with friends he speaks of his Beloved ﷾. And were he to receive an invitation to meet his Beloved ﷾, he would go walking on his head.

و الله ما طلعت الشمس و لا غربت
إلا و أنت في قلبي و وسواسي
و لا جلست إلى قوم أحدثهم
إلا و أنت حديثي بين جلاسي
و لا ذكرتك محزونا و لا طربا
إلا و حبك مقرون بأنفاسي
و لا هممت بشرب الماء من عطش
إلا رأيت خيالا منك في الكأس
فلو قدرت على الأتيان ذرتكم
سحبا على الوجه إو مشيا على الرأس

By Allah, the sun does not rise nor set,
But that You are in my heart and in my thoughts.
I do not sit in the gathering of friends,
But that You are my conversation among the people.
I do not remember You in grief or joy,
But that Your love is woven into my breath.
I do not intend drinking water in thirst,
But Your image I envision in the glass.
If I had the strength to come
I would, dragging my face or walking on my head.

Sincerity

When Muslims perform acts of worship [*'ibādāt*] they are motivated by the reward [*thawāb*] they will receive for their righteous deeds. Although this is a noble objective, the condition of the *'āshiq* is extraordinary. He does everything purely for the pleasure of his Beloved ﷻ.

Renewing Fervor

Allah ﷻ states:

كل يوم هو في شأن

Every day there is a new glory for Him. (55:29)

The beauty of the Beloved ﷻ gains new luster and charm with each passing day. In response the love in the heart of the sincere *'āshiq* also grows in fervor and adds dimensions. There is neither a limit to the beauty of Allah ﷻ, nor a limit to the intense love of the *'āshiq*. Thus, there remains no possibility of being attracted toward another. In the words of a poet:

My love is You, my companion is You,
My religion is You, my faith is You,
My body is You, my soul is You,
My heart is You, my life is You,
My Ka'bah, qiblah, masjid, pulpit, and Quran are You,
My worship- Hajj, alms, prayer, fasting- and adhan *are You,*
My remembrance is You, my reflection is You,
My pleasures are You, my existence is You,

My support, hopes, and trust are You,
My religion and faith are You, my honor is You,
My shame is with You and my glory is with You,
My pains, sorrows, tears, and laughter are You,

My pain is You and my respite is You,
My reasons for my happiness are You,
My reasons of comfort are You,
My beauty and youth are You,

O Farid,[14] *if only the Friend accepts you,*
Then you are the king and you are the ruler.

Establishment of the Night Vigil

The sincere *'āshiq* longs to intimately converse with his Beloved ﷻ. There is no better time for this than during the darkness of night. Therefore, it becomes the habit of the *'āshiq* to wake at the time of the night vigil [*tahajjud* prayer] to delight in its secrecy and to win over the Beloved ﷻ through his sighs and tears.

O sleeping Farid, awake and sweep out the masjid,
You are sleeping and the Lord is awake!
How will your friendship continue?

14 "O Farid" refers to the poet himself, *Hadrat* Baba Farid.

Humility

In spite of his nightly worship [*'ibādah*], a sincere *'āshiq* never feels he has done as much as he should. Even a dog remains awake at night guarding its master's home. As such, he does not regard spending the night awake as any great accomplishment.

You remain awake at night and are called 'Shaykh'
The dog that remains awake at night is better than you,
It eats bland, dry food and sleeps during the day under the tree shade,
It is better than you,
It leaves not the doorstep of its master, even if beaten a hundred times,
It is better than you,
O ingrate, you sleep upon a soft bed, whilst the dog sleeps on stone,
It is better than you.
Rise and win over your Friend,
Otherwise, the dog will have outdone you.

Another poet stated it differently:

By spending the nights awake, do not presume
That you have attained the ranks of the awliyā.
Brother, a dog spends its nights awake on guard,
It remains awake in exchange for a small morsel of food,
Whilst you have received thousands of blessings,
The dog has outdone you, O faqir, *hang your head in shame,*
Erase yourself until effaced, O faqir, *efface yourself until erased.*

Appreciation

The *'āshiq* even regards the sadness inflicted upon him by his Beloved ﷻ as better than any (worldly) happiness.

Even Your grief is very dear to me,
As it is something given by Thee.

The more the Beloved ﷻ rebukes the *'āshiq*, the more the *'āshiq*'s zeal increases. At times, in this state of immersion [in love], the *'āshiq* even proclaims, "Is there more?" [*Hal min mazīd?*]

Vitality

When Allah ﷻ bestows His attentive gaze, the world resounds with vitality. When this happens anyone could lose themselves.

> *Do not raise a finger against those entranced in their captivation,*
> *Look, is there any sense to be found even in a sensible one?*

Pleasure

An *'āshiq* finds such pleasure in talking about the Beloved ﷻ that his heart desires to speak of Him all the time. If he finds a friend whose heart is also full of such passion, then what remains? Both spend their time merrily.

Yearning

When the *'ishq* of an *'āshiq* is enflamed by the remembrance of the Beloved ﷻ, his heart yearns to see the Beloved ﷻ.

> *Lift the veil and reveal Yourself,*
> *I have come to see Your face.*

Struggle

The *'āshiq* tries to restrain his feelings and emotions. In this struggle, his entire life is spent.

> *Day and night is a struggle between desire, and suppressing desire,*
> *My heart agonizes me, and I agonize my heart.*

A STORY ABOUT PROPHET IBRAHIM

Once, when Prophet Ibrahim عليه السلام was grazing his flock of sheep, a man passed by loudly reciting the following words in praise of Allah سبحانه وتعالى:

سبحان ذي الملك و الملكوت سبحان ذي العزة و العظمة و الهيبة و القدرة و الكبرياء و الجبروت

Glorified is the Master of the Earthly and heavenly kingdoms. Glorified is the Honored One, the Exalted One, the Venerated One, the Powerful One, the Magnificent One, and the Omnipotent One.

When Prophet Ibrahim عليه السلام heard his Beloved سبحانه وتعالى praised with such beautiful words, his heart leaped in exultation. He requested the man to kindly recite the words one more time. The man asked what he would give him in return. Prophet Ibrahim عليه السلام replied that he would give half of his flock of sheep. The man complied and repeated the words. Prophet Ibrahim عليه السلام was so captivated by these beautiful words that he asked him to repeat the words again. The man asked what he would be given in exchange this time. Prophet Ibrahim عليه السلام replied that he would give the remaining half of the flock. The man complied and repeated the words for a third time. Prophet Ibrahim عليه السلام was so overcome with ecstasy by these words that he once again implored the man to repeat his words. The man responded, "You have nothing left. Now what will you give me?" Prophet Ibrahim عليه السلام replied, "O brother, I will tend your sheep forever if you recite these praises of my Beloved سبحانه وتعالى one more time." The man then said, "Ibrahim *Khalīlullah* [friend of Allah], I bring you glad tidings. I am an angel sent by Allah سبحانه وتعالى, who told me, 'Go and take

My name before My *khalīl* and see how much he values it."' *Subhān Allāh.*[15]

> ***Not for a moment could love be concealed,***
> ***when Your name was taken.***

THROWN INTO BOILING OIL

Once two Successors [*Tābi'īn*] were taken captive during battle. The enemy soldiers presented them before their king, a Christian. When the King saw the faces of the two *Tābi'īn* (rah), he found signs of bravery. He decided that instead of killing them, he would entice them to convert, thereby making them an asset for his army. They were promised luxurious lives, beautiful women, and high ranks in the army. They replied that the attractions of this transitory world held no importance in their eyes and that they would never leave Islam. Despite the King's persuasion they remained firm. When the King saw this he tried threatening them with severe punishment. He finally threatened to throw both of them into boiling oil if they did not convert. However, they remained steadfast and told the King to do as he pleased.

The King then ordered that a huge pot of oil be heated. Soon, the oil began to boil. He offered them one last chance to change their religion in order to save their lives. However, both of them adamantly refused. With a signal of the King's hand, one of them was flung into the pot. From the spurting oil steam arose and soon this Successor (rah) was charred beyond recognition. The King then looked toward the second Successor (rah) and noticed that tears were falling from his eyes. The King thought that perhaps he had become scared and was now ready to forsake his religion. Thus, in a sympathetic tone, the King said, "Your friend

---

[15] *Subhān Allāh* literally means, "Glory be to Allah."

did not accept my proposal. You see his outcome! Even now if you accept my offer, you will be saved." The Successor (rah) retorted, "O you wretched creature! Do you think that I fear death? Verily, it is not so!" The King asked, "Then why do you cry?" The Successor (rah) replied, "It occurred to me that I have but one life. And, if you throw me into this oil, it will end. How I wish that I had as many lives as the number of hairs on my body so that I could be thrown into this oil repeatedly and present each life as a sacrifice before my Lord, Allah ﷻ."

AN OLD *'ĀSHIQ*

Once Prophet Musa ﷺ was on his way when he saw an old man busy conversing with Allah ﷻ. Prophet Musa ﷺ overheard him saying, "O Allah ﷻ, I have heard that You do not have a wife. O Allah ﷻ, if You come to me, I would attend to You. I would serve You food, wash Your clothes, give You yogurt, and feed You butter. O, when You fall ill, who takes care of You?" Prophet Musa ﷺ explained to him that to use such words for Allah ﷻ was disrespectful, insolent, and contrary to the greatness of Allah ﷻ. The old man grew apprehensive and cried profusely, seeking Allah's ﷻ forgiveness. Allah ﷻ then sent divine revelation [*wahy*] to Prophet Musa ﷺ, "O My dear messenger! I sent you to bridge the distance between Me and creation, not to increase it."

> *You have come to present the Creator to creation,*
> *Not to create separation.*

THE LIFE OF *HADRAT* SHIBLI

During the Abbasid period Muslim rule had reached far and wide. Each territory had its own governor who handled its law and order and ran its internal affairs. Overall, most territories were governed honestly and justly, but a few territories needed reform. The Caliph of the time decided to gather all the governors at the capital to publicly honor and reward the successful governors and thereby motivate the others toward reform. A royal decree was issued and an invitation was sent for all the governors to gather at the capital on an appointed day.

When the day finally arrived, the Caliph assembled all of the governors in a special hall. Those who had proved to be good administrators were commended and rewarded, while the remaining governors were given constructive advice. At the conclusion of the meeting, the Caliph bestowed a robe of honor to each of the governors and invited them to a royal gathering the next day.

The following day the governors arrived dressed in their robes of honor. They enjoyed an extravagant feast of dishes and exotic fruits. After the meal, the atmosphere became lighthearted and the governors began to socialize. Even the Caliph appeared relaxed and content.

At this moment one of the governors sensed that he was about to sneeze and tried to suppress it. But, after struggling for a while, he sneezed two or three times. For a moment, the spirit of the gathering changed. Everyone looked towards him, and the governor sensed that perhaps some mucous was dripping from his nose. When everyone reverted their attention towards the feast, the governor discreetly wiped his nose with the sleeve of his robe. By the will of Allah ﷻ, at that very moment, the Caliph looked at him and saw him wiping his nose with the new robe. When he saw the robe being used to clean mucous from someone's nose, the Caliph became enraged. He severely chastised the governor for displaying such ingratitude toward his robe of honor and in the presence of the entire gathering, he stripped him of his robe and expelled him from the hall. The good spirit of the gathering had now died and the governors became afraid of facing a similar punishment. Sensing the change of atmosphere, the Caliph's vizier advised him to bring the gathering to an end. The crowd then dispersed and only the Caliph and his vizier remained in the hall, silently contemplating the unpleasant incident.

Soon thereafter, the doorkeeper entered and told them that the governor of the Nahawind Province sought their audience. The Caliph granted him permission to enter. Upon entering, the governor greeted him and asked whether a sneeze is a voluntary or an involuntary act. The Caliph, sensing the delicacy of the question, said, "What is the use of asking such a question? Go and attend to your work." However, the governor asked another question. "Regarding the governor who wiped his nose with the robe, was it necessary to disgracefully throw him out of your court, or could he have been given a lesser punishment?" When the Caliph heard this question, he replied, "I detect the implications of your questions. I warn you not to continue to ask such questions, otherwise you will regret it." The governor persisted, "O Caliph, I realized something through this incident. You bestowed someone a robe of honor and when he handled it with ingratitude you openly humiliated and expelled him. It occurred to me that the Most Generous Lord bestowed upon me the robe of humanity and sent me into this world. If I fail to pay due respect to this robe [of humanity], then on the Day of Judgment, Allah ﷻ will also disgrace and expel me in the same way." Saying this, he took off his robe and threw it on the table, adding, "I will first pay due respect to the robe of humanity, so that on the Day of Judgment I will be saved from humiliation." The governor thus spurned his governorship and left the hall. When he began reflecting about what he should do next, it occurred to him that he should seek the guidance of *Hadrat* Junaid Baghdadi (rah) to develop himself spiritually.

After some days of travel, he reached *Hadrat* Junaid Baghdadi (rah) and said, "*Hadrat*, you have been endowed with tremendous spiritual blessings. Please guide me to the same, whether for free or for a price." He replied, "If you are charged for it, you will not be able to afford it, and if it is given to you for free, then you will not value it." The governor said, "Then, I am prepared to do whatever you ask of me." He was told to remain there for a period of time and when his heart's reflection was found clean, he would receive the desired blessing. After a few months, *Hadrat* Junaid asked the governor about his past occupation. He replied that he used to be the governor of Nahawind Province. He was then told to go to the city of Baghdad and to open a shop selling sulphur. The governor did as he was told. Both the foul smell of sulphur and the daily bickering with the general public greatly distressed the governor. He completed a full year in this condition and presented himself to *Hadrat* Junaid saying, "*Hadrat*, I have completed one year." *Hadrat* responded, "Oh, so you were counting the days? Go and run the store for another year." This time the governor's mind was cleared to such an extent that more than a year passed, but he had not kept an account of time.

At last, one day *Hadrat* called him and told him that his second year had been completed. He responded that he had not realized how much time had passed. Then *Hadrat* handed him a beggar's bowl and told him to go to Baghdad to beg. The governor grew perplexed. He was told, "If you seek this blessing, do as you are commanded. Otherwise, return to the path from which you came." The governor immediately took the beggar's bowl and proceeded to the city of Baghdad. He saw people gathered in an area and extending his hand, he asked them to give something in the name of Allah ﷻ. Observing his face, they did not find it to be that of a beggar. They scolded him, "Lazy man! Aren't you ashamed of begging? Go and work for your keep!" When the governor heard these harsh words, he swallowed his anger and behaved like a true pauper.

Surprisingly, a whole year passed without his receiving anything. Wherever he begged he received the same treatment. This was a method for his spiritual reformation. *Hadrat* Junaid Baghdadi (rah) wanted to remove all vestiges of pride and arrogance from the heart of the governor. Thus, after a year of extending his hand before creation, he realized that he had no value; if one must beg, he should beg solely from the Creator. To attain this realization, it had taken an entire year of struggle.

One day, *Hadrat* Junaid Baghdadi (rah) called the governor and asked him his name. He replied, "Shibli." *Hadrat* then told Shibli that he may now sit in his gatherings. Hence, after three solid years of struggle [*mujāhadah*], *Hadrat* at last permitted him to attend his gatherings. As the heart of Shibli (rah) had already been purified, each and every word spoken by *Hadrat* Junaid (rah) illuminated his heart with *nūr* [spiritual radiance] and endowed him with much insight. Within a few months his spiritual state rose to such great heights that his heart was overwhelmed with love for Allah ﷻ.

Around this time, *Hadrat* Junaid (rah) called *Hadrat* Shibli (rah) and asked him, "Shibli, when you were the governor of Nahawind, you must have treated someone unjustly or deprived someone of their rights. You must make a list of those whose rights you violated." After three days, *Hadrat* Shibli had compiled a lengthy list. *Hadrat* Junaid (rah) explained that one's internal reformation was not complete until all his affairs were settled. He then told him, "Go and seek the forgiveness of all those people."

Thus, *Hadrat* Shibli (rah) went to Nahawind and sought the forgiveness of each and every person on his list. Some forgave him readily. Others said that he had disgraced them considerably and that they would not forgive him until he stood in the sun for extended periods of time. Still others would not forgive him until he worked as a laborer in their homes. And so it continued with everyone on his list. He fulfilled each condition according to the wishes of every person in return for their forgiveness such that two years had passed by the time he returned to Baghdad.

By now, it had been five years since he had first arrived at the sanctuary [*khānaqah*] for his spiritual reform. After enduring all these physical and spiritual struggles, the desires of his lower self [*nafs*] were annihilated and his ego erased. His spirit cried out "You, only You Allah ﷻ!" The mercy of Allah ﷻ descended, and one day *Hadrat* Junaid (rah) gifted him with spiritual connection [*nisbah*]. His way of seeing changed. His way of walking changed. His way of thinking changed. His chest became a treasury, and illuminated with the recognition [*ma'rifah*] of Allah ﷻ, he became a knower of Allah [*'ārif billāh*]. His heart was overcome with love for Allah ﷻ. The following are some significant episodes of his life.

Once *Hadrat* Shibli (rah) was sitting alone remembering Allah ﷻ when a seeker [*sālik*] passed by and said, "Connect me to Allah." *Hadrat* Shibli (rah) said, "To Allah?" The name of Allah ﷻ emerged from his lips with such reverential love that the young man's heart could not withstand it and he collapsed and died on the spot. *Hadrat* Shibli (rah) was arrested and charged with murder. When he arrived in court, the judge asked, "Shibli, did you kill a young man?" He replied, "Most certainly not. The boy asked me to connect him to Allah, and I only said 'To Allah but he could not handle these words." When the judge heard *Hadrat* Shibli (rah) say the word "Allah," he too felt a strange effect upon his own heart. As a result, he dismissed the case and honorably exonerated *Hadrat* Shibli (rah).

Whenever anyone took the name of Allah سبحانه وتعالى, *Hadrat* Shibli (rah) would place sweets in that person's mouth. Someone asked why he did this and he replied, "If I cannot fill the mouth of a person who takes the name of my Beloved سبحانه وتعالى with sweetness, what else can I do?"

Once people saw *Hadrat* Shibli (rah) furious, standing with a sword in his hand. When asked the reason for his strange behavior, he replied, "I will kill whoever takes the name of Allah سبحانه وتعالى in front of me!" When asked why, he replied, "I have discovered that people take the name of my Beloved سبحانه وتعالى negligently and in my eyes taking the name of the True Beloved سبحانه وتعالى negligently is disbelief [*kufr*]!"

One time while *Hadrat* Shibli (rah) was walking, a few boys began to follow him. Believing him to be insane, they started harassing him. He did not pay any attention to them and continued walking. One of the boys threw a stone striking him on the shin, which began to bleed profusely. Upon seeing this, a man scolded the boys and chased them away. He then approached *Hadrat* Shibli (rah) to tend to his wound. He was astonished to see that whenever a drop of blood fell from his wound onto the ground, it would form the word "Allah." Imagine how much love for Allah سبحانه وتعالى must have been infused in a body from which a drop of blood would form the word, "Allah"!

Once on Eid day, *Hadrat* Shibli (rah) wore black clothing. When people asked him why, he replied, "People are negligent of their Lord and due to their excessive sins their hearts have become as black as my clothes."

Once after performing *wudū* [ritual ablution], a divine inspiration [*ilhām*] entered *Hadrat* Shibli's heart (rah), "Shibli, are you going to My house (i.e. the *masjid*) after performing such a careless *wudū*?" *Hadrat* Shibli immediately turned back to repeat his *wudū*, but again received an inspiration, "Shibli, where will you go after leaving My door?" Suddenly in the state of *wajūd* [Divine Presence], he loudly exclaimed "Allah ﷻ." At this moment, another inspiration came, "Shibli, are you showing Me your fervor?" *Hadrat* Shibli then stood silently. Soon the thought arose, "Shibli, are you showing Me your patience?" Finally, *Hadrat* Shibli raised his hands in supplication and began to weep. In actuality, Almighty Allah ﷻ wanted to see *Hadrat* Shibli in humility.

On another occasion, Allah ﷻ inspired [*ilhām*] *Hadrat* Shibli's (rah) heart, "O Shibli, do you want Me to reveal your faults to the people so no one will ever again look in your direction?" *Hadrat* Shibli (rah) candidly said, "O Allah ﷻ, do You want me to reveal Your mercy to the people, so that no one in the world will remain who would prostrate to You?" Immediately, Allah ﷻ responded, "Shibli, do not tell anyone about Me, and I will not tell anyone about you."

These incidents demonstrate the profound love for Allah ﷻ that arises in one who erases the desires of his lower self [*nafs*] through intense spiritual struggle.

AN INNOCENT QUESTION

In his childhood, *Hadrat* Husain asked his father *Hadrat* Ali ؓ, "Do you love Allah?" He replied, "Yes." Then he asked, "Do you love my maternal grandfather (i.e. the Prophet ﷺ)?" He again replied, "Yes." He then asked, "Do you love my mother (i.e. *Hadrat* Fatima ؓ)?" Again, he replied, "Yes." Finally he asked, "Do you love me?" And *Hadrat* Ali ؓ replied, "Yes." *Hadrat* Husain ؓ innocently asked, "Dear Father, how have you combined so many loves in one heart?" *Hadrat* Ali ؓ explained, "Son, your question is an excellent one. The love I have for your maternal grandfather, for your mother, and for you is because Allah ﷻ has commanded all these loves. Hence, all these loves are in fact branches of love for Allah." Upon hearing this, *Hadrat* Husain ؓ smiled understandingly.

THE CONDITION OF SAMNUN MUHIBB

Hadrat Samnun Muhibb (rah) was a handsome young man who was deeply immersed in his love for Allah ﷻ. Once he was asked to deliver a lecture and share some words of wisdom. He spoke about the importance of love for Allah ﷻ. During the lecture, a bird came and sat on his shoulder. After a while, it moved down and sat on his lap. He continued talking about having love for Allah ﷻ while the bird continued fluttering about. Finally, at one point during his talk, the bird suddenly died on his lap. After this incident, people added the title, "Muhibb" [the lover] to Samnun's name.

UNABLE TO RECALL A NAME

Hadrat Maulānā Asghar Husain Kandhlawi's (rah) grandfather, *Shaykh* Ahmad Hasan (rah), was among the most pious people of his time. When the foundation of Dar al-'ulūm Deoband[16] was to be laid, *Hadrat Maulānā* Nanotwi (rah) announced that the first stone would be placed by someone who had never *committed* a major sin. In fact, this person had never even *made an intention* to commit one. People were astonished to hear this. *Maulānā* Nanotwi (rah) then requested *Shaykh* Ahmad Hasan (rah) to lay the first stone.

Shaykh Ahmad Hasan (rah) would absorb himself completely in *dhikr*. During the two years that his son-in-law stayed in his company, *Shaykh* Ahmad Hasan (rah) was never able to recall his name. Whenever his son-in-law passed, *Shaykh* Ahmad Hasan, (rah) would ask, "Who are you?" He would reply, "I am Abdullah.[17]" *Shaykh* Ahmad Hasan (rah) would respond, "All of us are Allah's ﷻ servants, but *who* are you?" He would reply, "I am Abdullah, your son-in-law." *Shaykh* Ahmad Hasan (rah) would then say, "Very good, very good." Every time he saw his son-in-law the same dialogue would occur, and this continued for two years. Allah's ﷻ name had permeated his heart to such an extent that he could no longer remember the name of anyone else.

THE SINCERE REPENTANCE OF JIGAR MURADABADI

Ustādh Jigar Muradabadi was a famous poet in his time. Although he was a drunkard early in his life, he was renowned for his exquisite poetry. Once he went to meet his friend Abdur Rabb Nishtar, the well-known politician. When the orderly at the office saw him dressed in simple attire, he denied him entry. *Ustādh* Jigar tried to explain that he was an old acquaintance of the governor,

---

16 Dar al-'ulūm Deoband, located in India, is one of the foremost institutes of Islamic learning in the world.

17 Abdullah is a name in Arabic which literally means, "servant of Allah."

but the orderly refused to listen. *Ustādh* Jigar then wrote two lines of poetry on a small piece of paper: "I have come to meet Nishtar, look into my *Jigar*." He asked the orderly to at least show his note to Nishtar. Upon reading the note Nishtar immediately recognized it to be written by *Ustādh* Jigar. He went out to personally welcome his old friend leaving the orderly dumbfounded. Such was the poetic excellence of *Ustādh* Jigar.

The turning point of *Ustādh* Jigar's life came after meeting *Hadrat* Khwaja Majdhub (rah) at a poetry recital. Jigar was deeply affected by the words of *Hadrat* Majdhub (rah). He was also surprised to find someone with a modern education and high status to be so imbued with love for Allah ﷻ. Jigar asked him how he had changed from his secular ways. *Hadrat* Majdhub (rah) told him that he had been influenced by *Hadrat Maulānā* 'Ashraf Ali Thanwi (rah) and offered to arrange a meeting with him if he so wished. Jigar agreed to meet *Maulānā* Thanwi (rah) but warned that he would drink wine, even in his presence.

Hadrat Majdhub (rah) requested *Hadrat* Thanwi (rah) to meet Jigar and told him about his drinking problem. *Maulānā* Thanwi responded that it would not be permissible for a drunkard to stay at his *khānaqah* [sanctuary devoted to spiritual reform]. However, he agreed to host *Ustādh* Jigar at his home where he could do as he pleased. So, *Hadrat* Majdhub brought *Ustādh* Jigar to the residence of *Maulānā* Thanwi (rah). A short period of time in the company of this friend [*walī kāmil*] of Allah ﷻ was enough to transform the heart of *Ustādh* Jigar. Jigar asked *Maulānā* Thanwi (rah) to make three prayers for him. The first was that he renounce drinking; the second that he adopt the *sunnah* of the Prophet[18] ﷺ as a way of life; and the third that he be able to per-

---

[18] The *sunnah* includes both the external (e.g. lengthy beard) and internal (e.g. mannerisms) acts of Prophet Muhammad ﷺ. Such was the

form *Hajj.* When *Ustādh* Jigar returned home, he renounced drinking and completely embraced the internal and external aspects of the *sunnah.* Shocked by this sudden and immense transformation in his life, people would come from far and wide to meet him. Regarding people's reaction to this change, Jigar composed a couplet about himself:

> *Let's go see the spectacle of Jigar,*
> *That infidel has become Muslim, is the rumor.*

Jigar's health deteriorated considerably due to his sudden abstinence from alcohol. His doctors advised him to leave this habit slowly. But, he replied that it was better to quit once and for all. If death were to seize him now, his repentance would be accepted, Allah willing, and he would be successful in the Hereafter. Love for Allah ﷻ had begun to overwhelm Jigar.

> *The miracle of my love is only this, O Jigar,*
> *Allah has overcome me and I have overcome the day.*

REMEMBERING [MURAQABAH] ALL NIGHT

Hadrat Maulānā Husain Ali (rah) was the authorized deputy [*khalīfah*] of *Hadrat* Khwaja Sirajuddin (rah). After the night prayer [*'isha*] at his *khānaqah*, it was common for *Hadrat* Husain (rah) to gather the seekers [*sālikīn*] to perform *murāqabah*[19]. They were permitted to leave if they felt tired. Thus, as the night progressed, people would leave the gathering of *dhikr. Hadrat* would raise his head and end his *murāqabah* after more than half the

---

understanding of the Companions [*Sahābah*] of the Prophet, the scholars, and the pious persons of this *ummah* until the present day.

[19] *Murāqabah* is a devotional exercise in which the *sālik* clears his mind of all foreign thoughts, reflects on the state of his heart, and focuses his concentration on the constantly descending mercy of Allah ﷻ.

night had passed, such that no one remained except him. He would then stand to offer the night vigil [*tahajjud*], thereby spending the entire night in the remembrance of Allah ﷻ.

My heart yearns for those leisurely days and nights,
When I would remain in reflection, thinking of my Lord.

HIS HAND WAS IN YOURS

A *shaykh* once came across a fire-worshipper occupied in worship. The *shaykh* explained that fire should not be worshipped as it is a part of creation and not the Creator, but the man refused to believe. The *shaykh* resolved to help him realize the truth and proposed that they make a fire and place their hands in it. He suggested that the fire would not burn the hand of the person whose belief was true. The fire-worshipper agreed to the proposal. The *shaykh* took hold of the fire worshipper's hand and placed both of their hands in the fire. After a moment, they realized that the fire did not burn either of their hands. The *shaykh* was baffled, as he had been certain that the fire-worshipper's hand would burn. At that moment, Allah ﷻ inspired his heart [*ilhām*], "How could We burn his hand, when it was held in yours?"

TWO GLAD TIDINGS

Once a Muslim and a Christian, both headed in the same direction, became traveling companions. When they were still two days away from reaching their destination, their provisions ran out. Both of them became worried and deliberated about what to do. The Muslim suggested that one of them should pray for food one day and the next day the other would pray for food. The Christian agreed and asked the Muslim to supplicate first. The Muslim withdrew to privately supplicate to Allah ﷻ. After a short while, a man came with a serving of hot food and laid it down before them. The Muslim was extremely pleased that Allah ﷻ had preserved his honor. After finishing their meal, they slept soundly during the night. The following day, it was the Christian's turn to supplicate and he appeared very confident. He retreated and prayed. After a short while, a man came with *two* servings of hot food. The Christian could not hide his happiness, but the Muslim was disturbed and did not care to eat the food. The Christian noticed this and said, "Eat, and I will give you two glad tidings." When they finished their meals the Muslim asked about the glad tidings. The Christian said, "The first glad-tiding is that I am accepting Islam. And the second is that when I supplicated, I said, 'O Allah ﷻ, if this Muslim has any standing in Your eyes, then give us food.' Hence, today Allah ﷻ has sent us a double helping of food in your honor."

Indeed, Allah ﷻ has such high regard for the sincere *'āshiq*, that Allah ﷻ accepts not only his prayers, but also the prayers of those who invoke the *'āshiq*'s favored standing [*wasīlah*]. According to hadith, the blessed Prophet ﷺ sometimes prayed to Allah ﷻ by invoking the standing of the Migrant Companions رضي الله عنهم [*Muhājirīn*]. After the passing of the blessed Prophet ﷺ, during times of drought the Companions رضي الله عنهم would turn to *Hadrat* Abbas رضي الله عنه and ask him to pray to Allah ﷻ on behalf of the community. After he passed away, they would request *Hadrat* Aisha رضي الله عنها to do the same.

WHO STOPS YOU FROM EXITING?

Once, a man offered to pay a worker to deliver some goods to his home. The worker agreed on the condition that on the way, if the time for prayer entered he would first offer his prayer [*salāh*] and then deliver the goods. The man accepted the worker's terms. After walking for some distance, they heard the call to prayer.

The worker told him that he was going for prayer as previously agreed. The man said that he would stand by the goods and told the worker to quickly pray and return.

The worker went into the *masjid* and became engaged in his prayer. Even though people began exiting, he remained immersed in prayer. After some time the man called out, "O you in there, it has been a long time! Who stops you from exiting?" The worker replied, "Sir, the One who stops you from entering is the One who stops me from exiting!"

Subhān Allāh such is the extraordinary condition of those who have *'ishq*. When they pray, it is as if they are intimately conversing with their True Beloved ﷻ.

A REMARKABLE SUPPLICATION

A man was on his way to the market when he saw someone trying to sell a bondwoman. She was very thin and, as a result, no buyers were interested. The man then purchased her for a nominal sum. When he woke up in the middle of the night, he saw her supplicating after the night vigil [*tahajjud* prayer]. She was saying, "O Allah ﷻ, I swear upon the love *You* have for *me*." The man reprimanded her and said, "You should not say that! But rather you should say, 'O Allah ﷻ, I swear upon the love that *I* have for *You*.'" Upon hearing this, the bondwoman became enraged and said, "Master, if Allah ﷻ did not love me, He would not let me spend the entire night on the prayer rug, while letting you sleep soundly." Saying this, she broke into tears and while weeping supplicated, "O Allah ﷻ, until now my situation was hidden, known only to Thee. My Creator, call me unto Thee as now Your creation has found out." Saying this, her soul was taken while sitting on her prayer rug.

THE ACTION OF HADRAT ALI AND FATIMA

Once *Hadrat* Hasan and *Hadrat* Husain became very ill and their condition failed to improve. *Hadrat* Fatima made a pledge to Allah that if her two sons regained their health, she and her husband would fast three consecutive days. In His mercy, Allah granted health to both boys and *Hadrat* Ali and Fatima began fasting. When the time to break the fast [*iftār*] arrived, there was only one serving of bread for both of them. At that moment, a beggar knocked on the door saying that he was a poor, hungry man who had come to their door with the hope that he might receive something to eat. Both husband and wife reflected and agreed that they could remain without food, but could not send a beggar away empty-handed. So they gave their bread to the beggar and broke their fast with only water. In the morning, they had only water to drink for their pre-dawn meal [*suhūr*]. That day, *Hadrat* Ali was able to earn enough for a single piece of bread. When the time for *iftār* drew near, once again there was a knock on the door. This time it was an orphan begging for food. Again, both thought that they could remain without food, but could not refuse an orphan. So they gave the orphan the bread and broke their fasts with only water for a second time. On the third day, they again had only water for *suhūr*. That day, *Hadrat* Ali managed to bring some food for *iftār*; however, it was barely sufficient for the two of them. This time a bondsman knocked on their door asking for food. After three consecutive days of fasting, both of them were very weak and hungry themselves. However, in their eyes it was not right to turn away someone who asked in the name of Allah, even though it meant enduring hardship. Love for Allah had permeated their hearts to such an extent that sacrificing their lives for Allah, let alone their food and drink, had become easy. So on the third night they again gave away what little food they had. Those who love Allah ﷻ are always ready to sacrifice everything for Him.

4

A COMPARISON BETWEEN LOVE [*'ISHQ*] AND INTELLECT [*'AQL*]

It is reported in a hadith that when Allah ﷻ created Adam ﷺ in the world of the spirits [*'ālam al-arwāh*],[20] He struck His right hand [i.e. His might] on the back of Prophet Adam ﷺ, causing offspring to emerge from his body. Their bodies were those of humans, but they were short in stature and their faces were glowing with radiance [*nūr*]. Allah ﷻ struck the back of Prophet Adam ﷺ again, and more offspring emerged, but their faces were devoid of the radiance that had shown on the others. Upon seeing all the offspring, Prophet Adam ﷺ asked, "O Lord, who are they?" Allah ﷻ replied, "All of them are your children."

Prophet Adam ﷺ looked at them again. The first time he had looked upon them as strangers, but this time he looked upon them as his own. He found that some faces were radiant while others were not. It is natural for a father to wish that all his

[20] "*'ālam al-arwāh*" literally means "world of the spirits." It refers to the place where Allah ﷻ created the souls of man and took a covenant from them, before giving them a physical presence in this world.

children be perfect, so Adam ﷺ asked, "Why did You not make them all alike, my Lord?"

Allah ﷻ replied, "Those with *nūr* are the inhabitants of Heaven and those lacking such radiance are the inhabitants of Hell." Allah ﷻ then addressed the children of Adam ﷺ saying,

أ لست بربكم

Am I not your Lord? (7:172)

All replied,

قالوا بلى

Verily, *You are* [*our Lord*]. (7:172)

During this exchange, there was no veil between Allah ﷻ and the children of Adam ﷺ.

On the occasion of this conversation, Allah ﷻ bestowed humanity with two gifts. By displaying His beauty [*jamāl*], love for Allah ﷻ [*'ishq*] was instilled in humanity. And by posing the question, "*Am I not your Lord*," humanity was endowed with the faculty of knowledge [*'ilm*]. For the inculcation of His love, Allah ﷻ granted humanity a beating heart; and for the acquisition of knowledge, Allah ﷻ gave human beings acute minds. Thus, the sustenance of the heart is love [*'ishq*] and the sustenance of the mind is sacred knowledge [*'ilm*]. Love alone leads to deviant innovations [*bid'āt*], and it is knowledge that restores a balanced equilibrium. Knowledge alone leads to arrogant pride [*takabbur*] and it is love that restores modesty and humility [*tawādu'*]. Love and sacred knowledge are inseparable; a complete person requires both blessings. If someone is deficient in either, then there is a danger of leaning toward extremes.

Throughout the ages, writers and poets have extensively compared and analyzed the relationship between love [*'ishq*] and intellect [*'aql*]. The true demand of love is to abandon everything at a single indication from the Beloved ﷻ and to strive to draw near to Allah ﷻ. On the other hand, the intellect seeks to avoid harm in every matter, seeking only that which seems beneficial. The intellect has a limit, whereas love knows no bounds. The intellect says that no path leads to the Beloved ﷻ, while love says I have returned having kissed the house of the Beloved ﷻ. A wise person is the one whose every footstep follows the dictates of the *'aql.* An enamored person is the one who, in the ardor of *'ishq*, is impatient to reach his destination. *Hadrat* Nisar Fathi says:

Many wise people have returned,
Only those madly lost in the ardor of love have endured the journey.

Searching for betterment is the quality of the *'aql.* On the other hand, restlessness and unease are the characteristics of *'ishq.* In the words of a poet:

Love's arduous passion has transcended many stations,
The intellect remains at the station where it started.

At times, the intellect discerns the path, but it does not have the endurance to attain its goal. It is then *'ishq* that lifts one on the wings of desire to reach the destination (i.e. nearness to Allah ﷻ).

Proceed beyond the intellect,
The light (of the intellect) is the lamp of the road, not the destination.

It is reported in a hadith:

أول ما خلق الله العقل

The first thing created by Allah was the intellect.

The function of the intellect is to distinguish between truth [*haqq*] and falsehood [*bātil*], and to preserve a balanced sense of reason. He who possesses intellect has a light with which he may find the way.

It is narrated that when the blessed Prophet ﷺ was describing the severity of the questioning in the grave by Munkar and Nakir,[21] *Hadrat* Umar ؓ asked, "O Rasulullah ﷺ, will the intellect be intact in the grave?" The blessed Prophet ﷺ replied, "Yes." *Hadrat* Umar ؓ then said, "Then there is no need to worry."

A hadith relates:

من لا عقل له لا دين له

He who has no intellect has no religion.

In this hadith, intellect refers to sound intellect [*'aql sālim*].[22] Thus, an intelligent person's religion is preserved because such a person can weigh his actions and distinguish between right and wrong. Another hadith regarding the intellect mentions:

أفلح من رزق له

That person who is blessed (with intellect) is successful.

---

21 Munkar and Nakir are the names of the two angels who interrogate a person in his grave shortly after death.

22 The *'aql sālim* is that intellect which is in accordance with the dictates of the Sacred Law and the primordial disposition of man [*fitrah*].

On the Day of Judgment, when the angels will ask the people of Hell [*jahannam*],

ألم يأتكم نذير

Did not anyone come to warn you (in the world)? (67:8)

They will reply,

لو كنا نسمع أو نعقل ما كنا في أصحب السعير

Had we listened and had we possessed intellect, we would not be among the people of Hell. (67:10)

The Glorious Quran says regarding the signs of Allah ﷻ:

إن في ذلك لأيت لقوم يعقلون

Verily, in it are signs for those of intellect. (13:4)

From the foregoing discussion, it is evident that distinguishing between benefit and harm and between doubt and certainty are the attributes of the intellect. Accordingly, a sound intellect is necessary to practice religion, and he who has a sound intellect is truly blessed. However, intellect alone is not enough. While the intellect is sufficient to acquire sacred knowledge, love is necessary for acting [*'amal*] upon one's knowledge. The intellect remains preoccupied in thought and reflection; action is dependent on *'ishq*.

The intellect is never free of thoughts and reflection,
Make love the basis of actions.

Traveling the path becomes difficult if one's footsteps follow the dictates of the intellect alone. The path leading to Allah ﷻ has many points where the intellect falters, causing one to stumble. However, if one rides the mount of love, one easily races along the path. And, endeavors that a person deems impossible are rendered possible by love.

One leap of love has completed the journey,
I had thought this Earth and sky to be boundless.

5

TRUE LOVE [*'ISHQ HAQĪQĪ*] AND METAPHORICAL LOVE [*'ISHQ MAJĀZĪ*]

True love [*'ishq haqīqi*] refers to love for Allah ﷻ, while metaphorical love [*'ishq majāzi*] refers to love for creation when it exists for the sake of fulfilling one's base desires. In short, true love is love for Allah ﷻ, Lord of the universe, and metaphorical love is love for creation. A more detailed explanation of these two types of love is given below.

METAPHORICAL LOVE [*'ISHQ MAJĀZĪ*]

The First Principle

In metaphorical love, the physical and external beauty of a man or woman is known as *husn*. It is *husn* that generates passion in youth. There is no greater influence in the material world than *husn*; it causes even highly intelligent people to act irrationally.

The Second Principle

Once an image of physical beauty becomes imprinted in a person's heart, that person is rendered helpless. *Shaytan* presents this image in such an attractive form that the person becomes absorbed with each glance.

يزيدك وجهه حسنا إذا ما زدته نظرا

The beauty of his face increases in your eyes, the more
you behold it.

The Third Principle

When smitten by *husn*, a person dies a spiritual death. Although he has eyes that see clearly, he views the faults of his beloved with admiration.

The Fourth Principle

Husn is ephemeral like the foam on the crest of an ocean wave. As a result, love that is based on physical form cannot be maintained for long.

The vicissitudes of life are wealth, beauty, and youth,
We ourselves have seen this, and history, too, bears witness.

Notwithstanding the ephemeral nature of *husn*, the lower self [*nafs*] is blinded by desire and fearlessly pursues its gratification regardless of the consequences.

The Fifth Principle

When unable to approach his beloved, a metaphorical lover [*'āshiq majāzī*] contents himself with the sight of his beloved from afar. He consoles his heart thinking that seeing from afar suffices.

The Sixth Principle

If the *'āshiq majāzī* gains the opportunity to be close to his beloved, then his *nafs* desires physical contact. Thus, the one who apparently claims to have true love reveals his deceit in this manner.

The Seventh Principle

When love degrades *husn* to fulfillment of lustful desires and selfishness, it loses its humanity. The truth is that no face is as attractive as it seems from a distance. No voice is as enchanting as it seems from afar. Is then the reality of physical attraction based on distance? If so, it would seem that it is better to keep a distance. Regardless, the metaphorical lover desires proximity to such an extent that he cannot be satisfied without physical consummation. Ask those who are drunk with lust and infatuation; even after consummation they remain unsatiated.

> *My life is still hanging around the noose,*
> *I swear, my love, even by gaining you, my thirst is not quenched.*

The Eighth Principle

Allah ﷻ, the Lord of the worlds, has placed an instinctive mutual attraction between men and women. However, He has also placed some restrictions and conditions for their relationships. If they live within these limits, they will be rewarded. If they exceed these limits, they will be punished. When purification of the soul [*tazkiyah al-nafs*] is not achieved, a man's mind is always preoccupied with thoughts of women. Similarly, women may be captivated by men. Even if the whole world praises the beauty of a certain woman, she herself can become infatuated with the physical beauty of one man. One of the greatest stories of love between a man and a woman is that of "Laila and Majnun". Due to its fame, *'ishq laila* [love for Laila] has become another term for *'ishq majāzī* [metaphorical love] as Majnun's love for Laila is symbolic of the love of worldly objects.

Majnun's real name was Qais. His story falls in the period of *Hadrat* Hasan ﷺ. Qais was deeply taken by Laila. He once met *Hadrat* Hasan ﷺ who said, "Qais, I have made peace with Amir Mu'awiyah ﷺ. I have handed the reigns of leadership to those suited for it." Qais kept silent for a while. *Hadrat* Hasan ﷺ asked him, "What are you thinking about?" He replied, "I was thinking that the governorship actually suits Laila." Upon hearing this *Hadrat* Hasan ﷺ stated, "You are crazy [*Anta Majnun*]!" and from then on he became known as "Majnun."

Once Majnun's father told him, "Because of you I have had to face considerable disgrace. The tales of your infatuation have spread far and wide. Come, I will take you to the Sacred Ka'bah. There, you can sincerely repent for your sins." When Majnun reached the Sacred Ka'bah, he clasped the shroud of the Ka'bah and supplicated:

إلهي تبت من كل المعاصي
و لكن حب ليلى لا أتوب

O Allah, I repent of all my sins,
But I repent not of my love of Laila.

When his father heard him say this, he looked angrily at him. Then Majnun recited another couplet:

رب لا تسبني حبها أبدا
و يرحم الله عبدا قال آمينا

O Lord, never remove my love for her,
And have mercy upon that person who says amen for my supplication.

Once a person saw Majnun kissing the feet of a dog. He asked Majnun, "Why are you doing that?" Majnun replied, "This dog has just come from the street on which Laila lives. That is why I am kissing its feet." What else can such an obsessed and insane person be called except for "Majnun" [crazy]!

Majnun used to circle the street where Laila lived, reciting the following couplets:

أطوف على جدار ديار ليلى
أقبل ذا الجدار و ذا الجدارا
و ما حب الديار شغفن قلبي
و لكن حب من سكن الديارا

I circle the walls of the house of Laila,
Sometimes I kiss this wall, sometimes I kiss that one,
It is not love for these walls that has infatuated my heart,
But the love of who lives within them.

Once, the mayor of the city thought that he should actually see with his own eyes the girl whom Majnun's love had made famous. When Laila was brought before him, he was astounded to see that she was just an ordinary girl without any extraordinary features, figure, or complexion. He said to her, "You are no prettier than any other girl." She retorted, "Keep quiet. You are not Majnun."

It is for this reason that the metaphorical lover claims that Laila should be beheld by the eyes of Majnun.

The Ninth Principle

If the metaphorical lover is to be executed for his love, then he desires that his beloved be present to witness the scene.

For the crime of loving you, I am being killed,
And there is much hue and cry,
You too, come upon the roof, and watch this strange spectacle.

The Tenth Principle

The metaphorical lover thinks that his eyes experience so much pleasure in looking at his beloved that his heart becomes envious. On the other hand, by thinking about his beloved, his heart experiences so much pleasure that his eyes become envious.

القلب يحسد عيني لذات النظر
و العين تحسد قلبي لذات الفكر

The heart envies the eyes - the pleasure of its observation,
And the eyes envy the heart - the pleasure of its reflection.

The Eleventh Principle

The metaphorical lover thinks that by merely seeing his beloved he is imbued with new vitality.

Even though I have become old, weak, and feeble,
The moment I behold you, I am young again.

The Twelfth Principle

The metaphorical lover finds every movement and action of his beloved attractive. Thus he believes her to correspond to his desires.

THE DECEPTION OF TRANSIENT BEAUTY

Those who are infatuated with the external appearance of a person are sorely deceived and worthy of pity.

Be lured not by transitory beauty,
Like an exquisite snake it strikes.

One aspect of human life is to fulfill the physical needs of the body. It is possible to satisfy these through marriage [*nikāh*]. Another aspect of human life is to fulfill one's base desires.

However, as there is never an end to such desires, it is impossible to fulfill them.

It is for this reason that in Islam, *nikāh* has been ordained as an act of worship [*'ibādah*] and even looking at non-relatives [*ghair mahram*] of the opposite gender is unlawful [*harām*]. Through marriage one may fulfill his or her physical needs and should thereafter remain satisfied and content. It is related in a hadith that if a man's gaze happens to fall on a woman and her beauty attracts him, then he should go unto his wife. Whatever that woman possesses, his wife possesses as well.

As far as figure, features, and complexion are concerned, there are many different creations of Allah ﷻ. With so many rivaling each other in beauty and with so much diversity, how many (beautiful creations) can one person actually obtain? If a person's gaze is tainted and his heart is full of lust, then even if he continues fulfilling his desires, he will tire but his desires will not end. Desire is a thirst that is never quenched. For this malady, there is no other cure except the fear of Allah ﷻ.

A man who was enslaved by his desires performed a pledge of self-rectification [*bay'ah*] at the hands of *Maulānā* Ashraf Ali Thanwi (rah). He wrote to his *shaykh* that he did not have the power to look away from women. He replied, "Strength is the name of that willpower which one can choose to use or not to use. If a person has the strength to perform an act but does not have the strength to abstain from it, then this is known as a sickness and not a power. Therefore, what you have is the *sickness* of looking at other women, and this must be cured." The man wrote again, "*Hadrat*, now I only look once, because the first glance is pardoned." His *shaykh* replied, "The first glance is pardoned if it occurs involuntarily. Otherwise, to look even once with intent is not permissible." The man wrote for the third time, "*Hadrat*, the creation of Allah ﷻ is a reflection of His attributes. Hence, I gaze upon the beautiful admiring them as reflections of Allah's ﷻ beauty." To this his *shaykh* replied, "Yes, the faces of the beautiful are indeed reflections, but they are fiery reflections that can incinerate. Remember, looking at such faces renders one worthy of the fire of Hell." The man wrote back finally saying that he had made sincere repentance [*tawbah*].

Once a man went to the *khānaqah* [sanctuary] of his *shaykh* for self-reformation [*islāh*] and resided there for a while. He was often busy in the duties of the kitchen. Sometimes a woman would come to clean the area and the man would gaze at her covetously. The woman noticed the attention she was getting and being chaste, she went to the *shaykh* and complained of his lustful glances. The *shaykh* grew perturbed and began to think of a means for this student's reform. In the meantime, the cleaning woman became ill with diarrhea. When the *shaykh* came to know of her condition, he sent a message for her to use a specific toilet so all her excrement would remain in one area. She did as he instructed. After a few days her condition improved, but she was still very weak and looked emaciated. When she returned to the kitchen to clean, the man looked away since she no longer appeared attractive to him. The woman informed the *shaykh* of his changed behavior. He called the man and, pointing to the specified bathroom, said, "Go look. Over there is your beloved." When the man went in to see, he found a pile of feces and excrement. Surprised, he asked how this pile of filth could be his beloved. His *shaykh* said, "At first when the cleaning woman would pass by, you would gaze at her covetously. When she became sick, it was this same filth that came out of her body. Then, when you saw her after her illness, you looked away. So it seems that your beloved was this heap of filth which had parted from her." The seeker [*murīd*] sought forgiveness and made sincere repentance [*tawbah*].

THE RESULT OF METAPHORICAL LOVE [*'ISHQ MAJĀZĪ*]

He who reveres the appearance of this world,
Will always have regret and sorrow.

The ultimate consequence of metaphorical love [*'ishq majāzī*] is the separation of the lover and the beloved and thus, disgrace in this world and the Hereafter. Whoever is in love with creation will have to separate or be separated from his beloved one day. And, whoever loves Allah ﷻ will be united with Him one day. As related in a hadith:

حب من شئت فإنك مفارقه

Love whomever you wish, but one day you will be separated.

Besides regret and remorse, one gains nothing in metaphorical love.

At the time of death, the true reality of life becomes manifest before everyone. All infatuations end. All illusions fade. This is the final end of metaphorical love. Whoever wishes to lead a successful life must abstain from it. Turning away from metaphorical beauty, some have changed their direction toward the true beauty of Allah ﷻ. The following are two such incidents.

In his youth, *Hadrat* Abdullah bin Mubarak ؒ was infatuated with a beautiful girl. One day she told him to wait outside of her house at night and that she would come out to meet him. He stayed awake, shivering in the long, cold winter night waiting for her. The girl did not come out to meet him as she had promised. When the call to prayer [*adhān*] was called in the morning, he felt humiliated. He thought to himself that he spent the entire night awake for the sake of a pretty girl, but did not experience anything except remorse and sadness. He lamented, "If only I had spent the whole night awake in the worship and remembrance of Allah ﷻ, then certainly I would have received some portion of His mercy and blessings." He then made sincere repentance [*tawbah*]. He later obtained a religious education, passed through the stages of purification of the self and the heart [*tazkiyah*], and became a leading scholar in the field of hadith.

Once, in a Muslim kingdom, a man was in love with the local princess. He was handsome and worked in the ruler's palace. Somehow he managed to relay his message of love to the princess. Having already heard praises of his beauty, she fell in love with him as well. Through a liaison, they would exchange messages, sharing their feelings of mutual affection. However, they could not find any way to meet inside the palace. Eventually, the princess thought of a plan. She sent a message to her beloved telling him that her father greatly respected pious people. She suggested that if her beloved were to leave his job, live on the outskirts of town, and engage himself in piety and worship for some time until he gained popularity, then she would be able to go out and meet him without restraints. He did as she suggested and settled near the edge of the town. He then adopted the *sunnah* of the Prophet ﷺ as his way of life and became occupied in remembrance [*dhikr*] and contemplation [*fikr*] of Allah ﷻ day and night. After a while, his piety became well-known among the people. The princess had been waiting for this opportunity. She asked her father his permission to go see this "holy man," making the excuse that she wanted to request his supplication [*du'a*]. Arriving at his dwelling, she left the entire entourage outside and went in alone. When her old admirer saw her, he said, "Sister, please go outside. How did you enter without permission?"

The princess reminded him that she was the same one whose beauty had enchanted him and who he had desperately ached to meet. She had come to see him so that they could finally meet and have this golden opportunity to be alone together. He turned his head away from her and said, "Sister, that time has gone. I had chosen this life of piety in the hope of meeting you. But now my heart abounds with the love of the True King. I desire not to even look in your direction."

TRUE LOVE [*'ISHQ HAQĪQĪ*]

Once, *Hadrat Maulānā* Inam-ul-Hasan (rah), the leader of the *Tablīghī Jamā'ah*, was going toward his quarters after giving a lecture. Some of his admirers were following behind him. When *Hadrat* turned and looked back, he saw that a man was crying as he was following him. After a few steps, he looked back again and saw the man following him in the same state. After a few more steps, he turned around again and saw that the man was still crying. *Hadrat* asked him consolingly, "Brother, why are you crying? Is there any way in which I can help you?" The man replied, "*Hadrat*, I am crying because of my love for you." *Hadrat* told him, "O servant of Allah تعالى, attach your love to the All-Living and Ever-Lasting, the One who never dies. What is the point in having love for an ephemeral being like myself? In due time, I will die. Brother, have love for that being who values each lover. How many admirers like you do I have? How can I show appreciation for all of you? Love that being who will appreciate your love in this world as well as in the next. Tomorrow, I will die, and then who will you love?"

Direct your love to the All-Living and Ever-Lasting,
Who exists forever and ever,
For you, Allah is the quencher of the thirst of your soul.

Understand that any love a person has for creation that is for the pleasure and content of Allah ﷻ is counted as love for Allah ﷻ. Thus, the love one has for his *shaykh* is purely due to the love one has for Allah ﷻ.

To have love for Allah ﷻ and to obey His every command is known as true love [*'ishq haqīqī*]. Through true love, success in this world as well as in the Hereafter is obtained. For those who are fortunate enough to receive even a single drop of true love, the value of this world completely diminishes in their eyes. Their eyes see through the attractions and allure of superficial appearances, and they consider them nothing but deception.

Once *Hadrat* Malik bin Dinar (rah) was going somewhere when he saw a pretty bondwoman wearing attractive clothing and walking haughtily. It occurred to him that this girl needed some advice. He approached her and asked, "O bondwoman, does your master wish to sell you?" She asked him why he wanted to know. He replied that he wished to purchase her. She thought that her stunning beauty and charm had made even this old man desire her. Amused, she told her servants that they should take this old man with them, to tell their master what he had said. So *Hadrat* Malik went with them. When they reached her master's home, the bondwoman laughingly boasted that even this old man had fallen in love with her after seeing her. Her master asked, "O old man, do you wish to purchase this bondwoman?" *Hadrat* Malik replied, "Yes." The master then asked, "How much would you pay for her?" Malik bin Dinar (rah) replied, "Two dry dates." The master was shocked when he heard this reply and responded, "Why such a paltry price?" The *shaykh* replied, "Because she has many faults. First, her beauty is temporary and one day will vanish. Second, soon she will age and her face will develop wrinkles such that no one will want to look at her. If she does not bathe for a few days a stench will emanate from her body, lice will fill her hair, a foul smell will come from her mouth, and her teeth will rot. If she does not comb her hair, she will look horrible. Finally, she is so unfaithful that today she is with you, and when you die, she will go to someone else." The slave's master said, "All that you say is true, but how do you come up with a price of two dry dates?" Malik bin Dinar (rah) replied, "I can obtain a slave whose beauty and charm is everlasting. When she smiles, rays of light emanate from her teeth. Her clothes are such that seventy thousand different colors shine forth from them. If she were to reveal the hem of her clothing from Heaven into the sky, the sun itself would seem dim in comparison. If she would talk to the dead, they would come to life. So faithful is she that I can see the waves of love arising in her heart myself. If she spits into bitter water, it would sweeten. I will receive this 'bondwoman' because of standing awake in the last portion of the night and offering two cycles [*rak'ah*] of the night vigil [*tahajjud*]." The master's eyes became full of tears and he said, "O *Shaykh*, you have transformed me." He then made sincere *tawbah*, and led a life of piety thereafter.

To dust the graves will turn,
The bodies of the beautiful.

A *shaykh* used to mention in his gatherings that he had attained love for Allah ﷻ through a woman. After hearing this, a man grew curious and decided to approach him. He asked, "O *Shaykh*, what is the story behind the woman you mentioned?" He then related the following story:

"Once I was sitting in my office working when a woman came and asked for a ruling [*fatwa*] as to whether a man who has one wife can marry again. I replied, 'Since a man is allowed up to four wives according to religious law [*sharī'ah*], how could I issue a ruling otherwise?' She said, 'This may be the ruling for other men, but as for my husband please write a ruling that he is not allowed to marry anyone else!' I declined to do so. However, she continued insisting and I kept refusing. Eventually, she sighed in exasperation and said, 'O *Shaykh*, the *sharī'ah* must be followed. Otherwise, I would raise my veil [*niqāb*], and you would see my beauty and charm. Then you would be compelled to write that any man whose wife is this beautiful should not be allowed to marry again!' Nonetheless, I still refused. She left, but she had ignited a burning love for Allah ﷻ inside me. If one woman can have so much pride in her beauty, then what about the beauty of Allah ﷻ? Would Allah ﷻ want that in His presence a man gaze with love at anyone else?"

AN IMPORTANT NOTE

To love those among creation that Allah ﷻ has commanded to love is in truth a completion of love for Allah ﷻ. A hadith states that the Prophet ﷺ used to supplicate:

اللهم إني أسألك حبك و حب من يحبك

O Allah, I ask of You Your love and the love for those who love You.

Therefore, to love the Prophet ﷺ is in reality to love Allah ﷻ. Similarly, love for the noble Companions [*Sahābah*] ﷺ, the family of the Prophet ﷺ, and the friends [*awliyā*] of Allah ﷻ also falls in this category. In addition, love for one's *shaykh* is also due to love for Allah ﷻ. There are certain limits to these loves of creation and to exceed these limits, or to fall short of them, is considered a sin. In essence, to have love for the Prophet ﷺ is a condition of one's faith [*imān*]. While, to love one's *shaykh*, parents, children, and spouse is the completion and perfection of one's love for Allah ﷻ. Thus, true love [*'ishq haqīqī*] is to love both Allah ﷻ and those among His creation that He has commanded us to love.

TRUE LOVE [*'ISHQ HAQĪQĪ*] AND METAPHORICAL LOVE [*'ISHQ MAJĀZĪ*] COMPARED

- True love is permissible and is an act of worship [*'ibādah*]; whereas metaphorical love is impermissible and sinful.
- True love secures one's religion as well as worldly-life; whereas metaphorical love destroys them.
- True love will one day result in meeting the Beloved ﷻ; whereas metaphorical love will one day result in separation from the beloved.
- True love illuminates the heart; whereas metaphorical love darkens it.
- True love breathes life into the heart; whereas metaphorical love brings it death.
- True love brings one respect and honor; whereas metaphorical love leads one to disgrace.
- True love's fervor is everlasting; whereas metaphorical love's zeal is temporary.
- In true love the lovers' final abode is Heaven [*jannah*]; whereas in metaphorical love the lovers' final abode is Hell [*jahannam*].
- True love's road is one on which all difficulties are endured easily; whereas in metaphorical love every difficulty is a punishment.

- In true love the lovers' faces glow with the freshness of spring; whereas in metaphorical love the lovers' faces cast the dreariness of winter.

6

THE CONDITION OF THE LOVERS OF ALLAH WHEN DYING

The sincere lover [*'āshiq*] passes his entire life preparing for death; for him, death is nothing more than a bridge leading to his Beloved ﷻ. Hence, when the moment of death draws near, he is overcome with happiness, as the days of trial and tribulation have come to an end.

I am grateful to Allah that I did not die,
Rather I have reached my Friend.

When the moment of death draws near, the friends and relatives of the sincere *'āshiq* call for a doctor, hoping a cure may be found for his illness. However, the condition of the *'āshiq* is such that for him there is no better remedy than death.

O my naïve friend, tell the doctor to leave my bedside,
There is no cure for the pain of love, except meeting the Beloved.

The condition of the sincere *'āshiq* at the time of death is like that of a tired beggar who has reached the door of the Generous

One ﷻ. Soon the door will open, and the Beloved ﷻ will fill the beggar's cup with abundant bounties and blessings.

The ultimate desire of a sincere *'āshiq* is to die during prayer [*salāh*] while in prostration [*sujūd*], or to die in Madinah Tayyibah, in order that his anxiety and restlessness may forever give way to peace and tranquility.

The condition of the lovers of Allah ﷻ is embodied in the following incidents:

Someone once exclaimed in front of *Shaykh* Najmuddin Kubra (rah), "Give your life! Give your life! Give your life!" He replied, "I have given my life! I have given my life! I have given my life!" Upon saying this, he passed away.

Once a sincere *'āshiq* left his home for Mecca, desiring to make *tawāf* of the Sacred Ka'bah. A strange condition overcame him when his gaze fell upon the Sacred Ka'bah and he passed away upon reciting the following couplet:

When you reach the lane of the Beloved,
Surrender your restless life,
Lest you may never again reach there to fulfill your desire.

The hadith scholar [*muhaddith*] Abu Dhur'a (rah) had memorized 100,000 hadiths. He could recite them from memory as easily as an ordinary person could recite *Surah Al-Ikhlās*.[23] Once, while teaching hadith to his students, he narrated the hadith that begins, "He, whose final speech is "*Lā ilāha illa'Llāh* [*There is no*

[23] *Surah Al-Ikhlās* is a short chapter of the Glorious Quran, chapter 112, which is easily memorized.

god except Allah]..." and then passed away. It was as if he was practically demonstrating the remainder of the hadith...that such a person will enter Heaven [*jannah*].

Khwaja Fariduddin Attar (rah) was once sitting in his shop when a *faqīr* entered and began to stare at the glass bottles lining the walls. Khwaja Fariduddin (rah) asked him, "What is the matter?" He replied, "I was just wondering how your soul will leave your body when it is trapped in so many bottles?" Khwaja Fariduddin replied, "My soul will leave my body the same way your soul will leave your body!" When the *faqīr* heard this, he immediately lay down on the floor, draped his shawl over himself, and said, "My soul will leave like this: *Lā ilāha illa'Llāh Muhammad ur-Rasūlu'Llāh*."[24] When Khwaja Fariduddin drew close and gently shook him, he realized that the *faqīr* had indeed surrendered his life to his Lord. This incident had a deep impact on him and his life completely changed. He then became the famous *Hadrat* Khwaja Fariduddin Attar (rah), author of the book, "Memoirs of the *Awliyā*."

Once, Siri Saqati (rah) and some *faqīr*s were gathered performing *dhikr*, when a sincere *'āshiq* came and asked, "Is there any place here where a person may die?" *Hadrat* was surprised upon hearing his question, yet indicated a nearby well and *masjid* and said, "Over there is a place." The person went to the well, performed ablution [*wudū*], performed two cycles [*rak'ah*] of *salāh*,

---

[24] *Lā ilāha illa'Llāh Muhammad ur-Rasūlu'Llāh* literally means, "There is no god except Allah, and Muhammad is the Messenger of Allah." It is a sign of acceptance from Allah ﷻ when a person passes away while reciting this *kalimah*.

and lay down. When the time for the next prayer arrived, people began to enter the *masjid.* Someone tried to awaken him for prayer, but discovered that Allah ﷻ had taken his soul.

When Mumshad Dinwari (rah) was on his deathbed, someone prayed, "O Allah ﷻ, grant Mumshad the bounties of Heaven [*jannah*]." Mumshad looked at him shockingly and said, "Every night for the past twenty years, Heaven was presented in all its beauty before me in my dreams, but not even for one moment did I divert my attention from Allah ﷻ and look in its direction."

When *Shaykh* Ibn Faridh (rah) was about to pass away, *jannah* was presented before him, yet he yearned only for the vision of his Lord, reciting:

إن كان منزلة في الحب عندكم
ما قد رأيت فقد ضيعت أيامي

If in Your esteem, the rank of love I attained
Has but this worth that I see now before me,
Then, indeed, have I wasted the days of my life.

A *shaykh* was in his dying moments and his mother was sitting beside him. His young daughter came to him, hoping that her father would talk and play with her. He remained lying quiet with his eyes closed, immersed in remembrance [*dhikr*] and reflection [*fikr*]. The daughter became upset and told her grandmother, "I am not going to talk to father." The grandmother said to her son, "Your little daughter is upset with you. Why don't you say something and appease her." He opened his eyes and asked, "What daughter? Whose daughter? It is my Beloved ﷻ that I have appeased, *Lā ilāha illa'Llāh Muhammad ur-Rasūlu'Llāh.*" As he said this, he passed away.

A Companion ﷺ was struck by a sword in battle and said, "I swear by the Lord of the Ka'bah, I have triumphed." As he said this, he was martyred.

Life was surrendered to Him who had given it in the first place,
The truth is that the right due to Him remained unfulfilled.

A young man passed away while immersed in *murāqabah* [spiritual reflection].

Near the time of his death, a *shaykh* recited,

يليت قومي يعلمون بما غفر لي ربي و جعلني من المكرمين

If only my people were to know that my Lord has forgiven me, and made me among the honored ones. (36:26-27)

When dying, another *shaykh* recited,

لمثل هذا فليعمل العاملون

Those who endeavor should strive for the like of this. (37:61)

The humble writer of these words once had a close friend who was pious, humble, and feared Allah ﷻ. He often performed *Hajj* and *'Umrah.* Whenever the name of Allah ﷻ was mentioned before him, tears would flow profusely from his eyes.

He was approximately eighty years old. During the month of Ramadan, while he was in spiritual retreat [*i'tikāf*] in the *Masjid* of the blessed Prophet ﷺ offering the late afternoon [*'Asr*] prayer in the *Riyadh al-Jannah*,[25] he passed away in prostration [*sajdah*], departing to meet his Lord. Thus, in one moment, he was graced with many blessings: dying in Madinah Tayyibah; dying in the *Masjid* of the blessed Prophet ﷺ; dying in *Riyadh al-Jannah*; dying with ablution [*wudū*]; dying during prayer; dying in prostration; dying while fasting; dying while in spiritual retreat [*i'tikāf*]; having his funeral prayer read in the *Masjid* of the blessed Prophet ﷺ; and being buried in *Jannah al-Baqi*.[26]

ذلك فضل الله يؤتيه من يشاء و الله ذو الفضل العظيم

This is the grace of Allah, He bestows it upon whom He wishes. Verily, Allah is the Most Gracious. (57:21)

When *Shaykh* Khwaja Moinuddin Chishti Ajmeri (rah) passed away, people saw the following written on his forehead:

هذا حبيب الله مات في حب الله

This is Allah's beloved, who passed away in love with Allah.

---

[25] *Riyadh al-Jannah* is the portion of the *Masjid* of Prophet Muhammad ﷺ that will be a part of Heaven in the Hereafter.

[26] *Jannah al-Baqi* is the graveyard located in Madinah where many Companions [*Sahābah*], Successors [*Tābi'īn*], and righteous believers [*sālihīn*] are buried.

7

THE CONDITION OF THE LOVERS OF ALLAH IN THEIR GRAVES

At the time of death, the lovers of Allah ﷻ are showered with the blessings of Allah ﷻ, experiencing extraordinary and wondrous states in their graves.

They entered their graves with the dye of love for Allah,
Into darkness like the night, they took along their lamps.

Several incidents in this regard are given below:

The angels asked *Shaykh* Yahya bin Mu'adh Razi (rah) in his grave, "What have you brought?" He replied, "Verily, great is the statement of my master, the blessed Prophet ﷺ:

الدنيا سجن المؤمن

The world is a prison for the believer.

Tell me, what can a prisoner bring from a prison?" The angels left upon hearing this reply, and his grave was made into a garden.

A person saw Bayazid Bustami (rah) in a dream and asked him, "What transpired in your grave?" *Hadrat* Bustami replied, "The angels came and asked, 'O old man, what have you brought?' I replied, 'When someone arrives at the door of a king it is not asked what he has brought, but rather what he has come to receive.'" The angels became happy upon hearing this reply.

After passing away Rabia al-Basriyyah (rah) appeared in a person's dream. This person asked her (rah) what happened after she passed away. She said, "The angels came and began to ask, 'Who is your Lord [*Man Rabbuki*]?' I told them to go to Allah سبحانه وتعالى and say on my behalf, "O Allah سبحانه وتعالى, Your creation is so vast yet You did not forget one old woman. I have no one but You, how could I forget You?"

The angels asked *Shaykh* Junaid Baghdadi (rah) in his grave, "Who is your Lord?" He replied, "My Lord is He who commanded the angels to prostrate before Prophet Adam عليه السلام." The angels were stunned by this reply and went away.

After passing away, *Hadrat Shaykh* Abdul Qadir Jilani (rah) appeared in a person's dream and was asked, "What happened after passing away?" He said, "The angels asked me, 'Who is your Lord?' I replied, 'It is surprising that you have descended from the *Sidrah al-Muntaha*[27] and have not forgotten Allah ﷻ. Should it be that I, who have descended only four feet, should forget everything?' Thereafter the gates of Allah's ﷻ mercy were opened and my grave was transformed into a garden."

It is narrated in a hadith that when a believer is buried, Allah ﷻ tells the angels, "Here is a servant of mine, who having come from the material world [*dunyā*], is tired. Tell him:

نم كنومة العروس

Sleep the sleep of a newlywed bride.

Here the scholars of hadith have noted a subtle point. The narration does not state, "Tell him: 'Sleep peacefully'," but rather, "Tell him: 'Sleep the sleep of a newlywed bride.'" When a bride sleeps, none other than her beloved awakens her. Similarly, the believer sleeping in his grave will also be awakened by none other than his True Beloved ﷻ on the Day of Judgment. When a bride awakens, she sees the smiling face of her husband. And, when a sincere *'āshiq* awakens on the Day of Judgment, he will behold Allah ﷻ smiling upon him.

---

[27] *Sidrah al-Muntaha* is a place located in the Seventh Heaven.

8

THE CONDITION OF THE LOVERS OF ALLAH ON THE DAY OF JUDGMENT

According to a hadith, some people will rise on the Day of Judgment in such a state that upon seeing Allah ﷻ, they will smile, and upon seeing them, Allah ﷻ will smile. A voice will then be heard:

يأيتها النفس المطمئنة ارجعي إلى ربك راضية مرضية فادخلي في عبدي و ادخلي جنتي

O you contented soul! Return unto your Lord, well pleased [*yourself*] *and well pleasing* [*unto Him*]. *Enter you, then, among My honored servants, and enter you into My Paradise.* (89:27-30)

Those who love Allah ﷻ, and moreover, those who love one another for the sake of Allah ﷻ will be granted sanctuary under the shade of the Throne [*'Arsh*] of Allah ﷻ. On that day there will be no shade except the shade of the *'Arsh*. For ordinary people, the Day of Judgment will last 70,000 years; whereas, for the lovers, it will last only the duration of the two *sunnah* cycles [*rak'ah*] before the morning [*fajr*] prayer. They will stroll upon hills of musk and behold the beauty [*jamāl*] of the True Beloved سبحانه وتعالى.

> *The lovers will have naught to do*
> *With the tribulations of the Day of Judgment*
> *No concern will the lovers have*
> *Other than beholding the beauty of their Beloved.*

Some lovers will be so absorbed in their yearning for Allah سبحانه وتعالى that they will rush to the gates of Heaven [*jannah*] and ask the gatekeeper, the Angel Ridwan عليه السلام, "We were told in the world [*dunyā*] that in Heaven one is granted the beatific vision of Allah سبحانه وتعالى." The Angel Ridwan عليه السلام will ask Allah سبحانه وتعالى, "O Lord, the scales of justice have yet to be weighed, yet these people seek entry into Heaven?" Allah سبحانه وتعالى will address them, "O my servants, you have still to account for your deeds, yet you wish to enter Heaven?" The lovers will respond, "O Lord, Most Generous, You know well that we turned our backs on the material world, and devoted ourselves only to You. Our hearts desired not the bounties of the world and we always remained content. We loved You and worshipped You throughout the nights, our foreheads in prostration. We prayed and supplicated unto You from the depths of our hearts. We restlessly passed the nights away, longing to attain Your pleasure. At the time of our death we had nothing in our hearts but love for You." Allah سبحانه وتعالى will then address the Angel Ridwan عليه السلام, "Ridwan! These are my lovers, what reckoning can there be of them? Open the gates of *jannah* and let them enter without having to account for their deeds."

According to a hadith, on the Day of Judgment, Allah سبحانه وتعالى will express regret to those lovers who faced adversity in the material world [*dunyā*] and lived in abstinence, remaining poor and hungry. Allah سبحانه وتعالى will commiserate Himself before them, just like a friend feels bad in front of another friend for not giving him a gift.

On the Day of Judgment, the lovers will be gathered near the watering place [*hawd*] of *Kauthar.* The most beloved of Allah ﷻ and the mercy unto the worlds [*rahmah lil-'alamīn*], the blessed Prophet ﷺ, will fill cups of water for them to drink. He will recognize each of his followers by the *nūr* [spiritual radiance] shining forth from the limbs that they used to wash in ablution [*wudū*]. Even the angels will be pleased when they see these people as the followers [*ummah*] of Prophet Muhammad ﷺ.

When they reach the plains of judgment,
The dazzling angels will rise and proclaim,
The servants of the servants of
The servants of Muhammad have arrived!

The hardships of the Day of Judgment will fall upon the disbelievers [*kuffār*], those who associated partners with Allah ﷻ [*mushrikīn*], the hypocrites [*munāfiqīn*], and the sinners [*fāsiqīn*]. The lovers will cross the bridge [*sirāt*] over Hell as fast as the speed of wind. The heat of hellfire will be cooled by the light [*nūr*] of their faith [*imān*] such that Hell itself will cry out and request the lovers to pass quickly, lest their faith extinguish its fires.

On the Day of Judgment, Allah ﷻ will grant the lovers the right of intercession [*shifā'ah*]. They will take many sinners along with them into Heaven. The lovers will not be subjected to the rigors of the Day of Judgment and they themselves will be a means of delivering others from it. A radiant *nūr* will shine in front of them, leading them to the doors of Heaven:

و سيق الذين اتقوا ربهم إلى الجنة زمرا

And those who feared their Lord will be led into Heaven in droves. (39:73)

On the Day of Judgment, Allah ﷻ will have a special regard for those who instilled love for Allah ﷻ in the hearts of others. On that day, wealth and children will be of no use:

يوم لا ينفع مال و لا بنون إلا من أتى الله بقلب سليم

The day in which neither wealth nor children will benefit any man, save he who comes to Allah with a pure heart.
(26:88-89)

Those believers who passed this ephemeral abode as poor and indigent will be treated as honored guests on the Day of Judgment. It is reported in a hadith that the blessed Prophet ﷺ used to supplicate:

اللهم أحيني مسكينا و أمتني مسكينا و احشرني في زمرة المساكين

O Allah, let me live as an indigent and die as an indigent. Raise me among the indigent on the Day of Judgment.

O Allah, grant me a heart imbued with love for Thee,
And may Thy mercy always descend upon my heart,
Grant me a heart that is so absorbed in love for Thee that
I may be oblivious to the pandemonium of the Day of Judgment.

9

THE SIGNS OF A SINCERE LOVER

The daily rising of the sun is itself proof of the existence of the sun. Similarly, the scent of a fragrance indicates its presence:

> *Musk emanates a scent by itself,*
> *It needs not the seller to describe it.*

Several signs by which a sincere *'āshiq* may be recognized are given below:

Sign Number One

A sincere *'āshiq* can be recognized by the essential nature of his being [*dhāt*]. When the blessed Prophet ﷺ was asked about the signs of the friends of Allah ﷻ [*awliyā*] he replied:

الذين إذا رؤوا ذكر الله

Those people who - when they are seen - Allah is remembered.

The signs of a sincere *'āshiq* are found in his radiant face and noble demeanor, such that even a stranger can recognize an *'āshiq* upon seeing him. Even though his appearance seems modest, an intelligent person recognizes the sincere *'āshiq* at first glance. Hearts are attracted to a sincere *'āshiq* as strongly as metal is attracted to a magnet.

Sign Number Two

The Glorious Quran mentions three signs of the lovers:

إذا ذكر الله وجلت قلوبهم و إذا تليت عليهم آيته زادتهم إيمانا و على ربهم يتوكلون

Those people whom, when Allah is mentioned, their hearts tremble with fear, and if a verse is recited unto them, their faith is strengthened [*thereby*]. *And they trust and rely upon their Lord.* (8:2)

The first sign is that when Allah ﷻ is mentioned before them, their hearts tremble with fear. A poet once said:

Not for a moment may love be concealed,
when Your name is taken.

The second sign is that when the words of the Beloved ﷻ are recited before them, their faith [*imān*] is strengthened. The third sign is that they have trust and reliance [*tawakkul*] upon Allah ﷻ.

Sign Number Three

It is reported in a hadith that once the blessed Prophet ﷺ was asked about the signs of a true believer. He replied:

تجافي عن دار الغرور و الإنابة إلى دار الخلود و استعداد للموت قبل نزوله

Withdrawal from the abode of deceit (the material world); inclination toward the eternal abode (the Hereafter); and readiness for death before its arrival.

The first sign is that despite its attractions and abundant goods, the material world [*dunyā*] is unable to attract a believer's heart and he remains unaffected by the glamour of this world.

Withdrawn have I from the affairs of the world, O Lord,
What heights of pleasure and serenity are to be found,
Once the dunyā *is extinguished from one's heart.*

The second sign is that his attention is focused toward the everlasting life [*ākhirah*]. The third sign is that he prepares for death before it comes, just as an *'āshiq* prepares to meet his beloved. It is reported in a hadith:

الموت جسر يوصل الحبيب إلى الحبيب

Death is a bridge which brings one friend to another.

Sign Number Four
According to a famous Arabic saying:

لو كان حبك صادقا لأطعته إن المحب لما يحب مطيع

If your love is true, then certainly you will obey him (your beloved), for verily the lover is not but obedient to his beloved.

A sincere *'āshiq* always obeys his Beloved ﷺ. Truly, this is the greatest sign of all. The entire life of the sincere *'āshiq* conforms to the sacred law [*sharī'ah*] and the way [*sunnah*] of Prophet Muhammad ﷺ. Once a watermelon was presented before *Hadrat* Bayazid Bustami (rah). He asked, "What is the Prophetic way [*sunnah*] to cut and eat this?" None of the scholars gathered were able to answer and as a result *Hadrat* declined to eat it, lest he eat it in a manner contrary to the *sunnah*. Although it is permissible in the *sharī'ah* to eat such a thing in whatever way one may wish, for the lovers, adhering to the *sunnah* of the blessed Prophet ﷺ is the only way of life.

Sign Number Five

A distinct sign of a sincere *'āshiq* is that he does not care for anything other than his Beloved ﷻ. In the *sharī'ah*, just as loving Allah ﷻ is an act of worship, so too is having disdain for everything other than Allah ﷻ. The heart of a sincere *'āshiq* is empty of love for everything other than Allah ﷻ. The sword of "*Lā ilāha illa'Llāh*" has severed all relations. The heart of one immersed in metaphorical love [*'ishq majāzī*] loves none other than its beloved. What then can be said of those who attain the lofty rank of divine love [*'ishq haqīqī*]?

Once a man saw a beautiful woman and exclaimed, "I am in love with you and want only you!" In reply she said, "My sister is coming behind me, and she is even prettier than me." As the man turned to look back, the woman struck him on the head with her shoe saying, "You liar! If truly you loved *me*, then what need was there to look in any other direction?"

A person once proclaimed love for Queen Zubaida. Zubaida called him and said, "Take however large a sum you wish from the treasury, but proclaim not that you love me." The man asked, "How much money are you offering me?" Zubaida replied, "Ten thousand *dinār*s." Upon hearing this, he fell quiet, silencing his claim of love. Zubaida told the Caliph, Harun al-Rashid, "This man is a deceiving liar. Have him punished." After receiving a sound thrashing, the man regained his senses.

Sign Number Six

Hadrat Khwaja Uthman Haruni (rah) used to say that there are three characteristics that mark a sincere *'āshiq*: he is humble like the Earth; he has mercy like the sun; and he is generous like the ocean.

Sign Number Seven

According to a poet:

> *Know that the signs of an* 'āshiq *are three,*
> *A pale complexion, deep sighs, and wet eyes.*
> *And that the signs of a traveler* [sālik] *on the path* [tarīqah]
> *Are three as well - eating less, speaking less, and sleeping less.*

The first characteristic of a sincere *'āshiq* is a pale and yellow complexion. Intense spiritual training and abundant devotions often have such an effect. The second characteristic is deep sighs of longing, due to separation from the Beloved ﷻ. The third characteristic is that the eyes remain wet with tears, as the restlessness of the heart is released through the eyes. The fourth characteristic is to eat little. A sincere *'āshiq* does not succumb to gluttonous pleasures; rather he eats merely to get by. The fifth characteristic is to speak little. The person whose inner soul converses with his Beloved ﷻ has no desire to engage in idle conversation. The majority of the *awliyā* speak only out of necessity. Otherwise it is their practice to remain silent.

Once someone asked of *Hadrat* Khwaja Baqi Billah (rah), "*Hadrat*, you are always silent. If you were to speak some words of advice, people would benefit." *Hadrat* replied, "Those who benefit not from my silence will be unable to benefit from my words."

The sixth characteristic of a sincere *'āshiq* is to sleep little. His nights pass in remembrance [*dhikr*] and worship. A *shaykh* used to say, "A seeker [*sālik*] should refrain from sleeping until sleep overcomes him so greatly that he collapses or comes close to collapsing." A sincere *'āshiq* spends his entire life restlessly seeking his Lord through worship, until he attains the state:

و اعبد ربك حتى يأتيك اليقين

And worship your Lord until certainty comes over you. (15:99)

10

LOVE FOR ALLAH IN PRESENT TIMES

In the present era, people have become so preoccupied in satisfying the needs of their bodies that they are oblivious of Allah ﷻ. Everyone is prey to the deceits of their base desires [*nafs*] and is absorbed in submitting to whatever these desires dictate.

> *I found no one whose heart's condition was sound and true,*
> *I found worshippers of idols, but found not a worshipper of Allah.*

It seems that those chests that used to glow like burning red coal due to an intense love for Allah ﷻ are today no more than heaps of ash. People have become unfamiliar with the inner reality [*haqīqah*] of worship. They attend the prayer, yet remain absent in spirit. They abstain from food and drink while fasting, yet they do not wholly refrain from sin. Their state of fasting extends to their stomachs, yet fails to encompass their eyes.

> *The frenzy of love no longer remains,*
> *That (passionate) heart, that yearning, are no more,*
> *Prayer, fasting,* qurbānī, *and Hajj all remain,*
> *But love for You is no more.*

There was once a time when young men and women used to awaken in the last portion of the night to prostrate before Allah ﷻ and to warm their hearts with the *dhikr* of "*Lā ilāha illa'Llāh*." Today, the faces of those who restlessly passed the night away, yearning for the Beloved ﷻ, are seen no more.

Those believers whose gaze could pierce the hearts are no longer to be found.

The hearts trembled in the breast due to your gaze,
Alas, the devotion of the pious is no longer among us.

It is for this reason that the Muslims of today are overpowered by cowardice, so much so that they are afraid even of the dark. They fear going to a desolate place. Even the clawing of a cat frightens them. It is amazing that a Muslim who is scared of the mere ruffling of a window curtain, does not fear Allah ﷻ. It is unfathomable why the fear of creation constantly preoccupies man's heart; fear that one's employer may become angry, fear that one's wife may become angry, fear that if one speaks the truth then so-and-so might become angry, or fear that if a marriage is celebrated in a simple manner then relatives may become angry. The reality is that until the heart is purified and one's gaze becomes pure, a person cannot become courageous.

The heart is free from passion for Allah, the gaze is not pure,
What surprise is it then, that you are not courageous?

Our predecessors [*aslāf*] safeguarded the respect and honor of women at a time when people used to sell their own sisters. They prostrated before Allah ﷻ at a time when people used to bow before others. They opposed tyranny at a time when people proudly committed oppression. The Muslims of today bear only a superficial resemblance to them. In terms of spiritual piety, we are as far from them as the sky is from the Earth. They were seekers of Allah ﷻ and we are seekers of the material world [*dunyā*]. They annihilated their base desires [*nafs*], while we submit to ours. They were people who strove on the Straight Path, while we passively draw near to our graves. They were kind and welcoming toward one another, whereas we have anger and spite toward one another. They maintained their honor and dignity, whereas we have lost all respect. Their hearts were full of love for Allah ﷻ while our hearts are devoid of such love. Our disgraceful condition has reached such an abyss that even the supplications [*du'āt*] of our pious ones have lost effect, save those that are accepted by the will of Allah ﷻ.

> *I spent one night crying profusely before Allah,*
> *Asking Him why the Muslims have become so disgraced,*
> *A voice said, 'You know well that while the Muslims have hearts,*
> *Their hearts are devoid of the Beloved.'*

Those who have purified their hearts are deeply concerned with the fallen state of the Muslims and earnestly supplicate to their Lord to rectify this condition.

Today, there are very few people who remain awake throughout the night in acts of worship [*'ibādāt*], and there are even fewer who use this time to win over the Beloved ﷻ through tears and desire. The first portion of the night is indulged in fun and entertainment and the last portion is spent sleeping and dreaming. To sleep soon after the night prayer [*'ishā*] is a *sunnah*. Nowadays, many shops begin to get crowded after the night prayer. In particular, shops where food and drink are sold remain open until two in the morning. When it is two o'clock, and the time of the night vigil [*tahajjud*] begins, these people head for their beds and then miss the morning prayer [*fajr*]. Many people have passed years without witnessing dawn or sunrise. The person who claims to be unable to wake up for the morning prayer at dawn, regularly awakens shortly thereafter eager for breakfast.

If a person is offered a wage of one hundred dollars to remain awake the entire night and stand guard, he will readily sacrifice his night's sleep. Yet on the night he is off-duty, if he is asked to stay awake for half the night and pray the night vigil [*tahajjud*], he will reply that he is unable to wake up. Thus, in his eyes, the value of *tahajjud* is not even fifty dollars, even though in the last portion of the night the angels announce in the sky:

من سائل فأعطى له

Is there anyone asking for something that it may be granted to him?

From the Giver there is an offer, but the one who could have accepted it is snoring loudly, deep in sleep.

Once a man was offering his prayer when a woman with her head uncovered passed in front of him, crying and screaming. The man quickly completed his prayer and admonished her, "O servant of Allah ﷻ, are you blind? I was praying and you disrespectfully passed in front of me." The woman replied, "If you permit, I would like to tell you something." The man said, "Fine." She said, "My husband divorced me, and because of the love I had for him, I became deranged and did not notice that I passed in front of you. But, what kind of sincere *'āshiq* are you that even in your prayer you are aware of who passes in front of you? Do you offer prayer whilst looking at your Master or at women passing in front of you? What of the command:

أن تعبد الله كأنك تراه

...that you worship Allah as if you are seeing Him.

In our time, there is an increasing tendency in the Friday prayer [*jumu'ah*] toward journalistic talks on current events. Indeed, while our pious predecessors prepared their Friday sermons from the books of Quranic exegesis [*tafsīr*] and hadith, today the Friday lecture is prepared from newspapers.

> *Every word of the speaker's lecture is entertaining,*
> *But alas, there is no love for the Creator in his eyes,*
> *Nor the radiance of certainty of faith on his face.*

Nowadays, the sanctuaries devoted to spiritual reform [*khānaqahs*] are also becoming empty. Even those persons connected to spiritual guides [*mashā'ikh*] do not have time to perform *dhikr*. It has become increasingly difficult to recite invocations [*tasbīhāt*] or to fill one's heart with spiritual radiance [*nūr*].

We should thank Allah ﷻ that even today some people remain who are grieved by the lack of love for Allah ﷻ. Their existence itself is a blessing.

11

HOW TO ATTAIN LOVE FOR ALLAH

In order to attain true love [*'ishq haqīqī*] for Allah ﷻ, the following principles must be established:

SINCERE YEARNING [*TALAB*]

The foremost condition of attaining love for Allah ﷻ is to sincerely crave such love. A person may acquire the material world [*dunyā*] passively, but true love [*'ishq*] is a treasure; therefore it cannot be acquired unless one actively seeks it.

> *I am humbled by my abaseness, and in awe of Your exaltedness,*
> *Yet, what can I do of my heart, still it desires to reach You.*

A person may be made of dust and earth, yet far does his gaze travel when he desires the countenance of the True Beloved ﷻ.

> *Where is this* [*lowly*] *heart, that it may desire to attain the Beloved?*
> *Where is the King of the beautiful? And how far are we?*

When a person sits to remember Allah ﷻ, but discovers his heart full of heedlessness and neglect, he should recite the following prayer to himself:

> *O Beneficent One, have grace upon me, I am in great agony,*
> *I am sitting before You, yet still I remain veiled.*

A person must make firm intention in his heart to acquire true love for Allah ﷻ and must be prepared to sacrifice everything for this goal.

RELINQUISHING WORLDLY PLEASURES

To attain the True Beloved ﷻ, it is imperative that one abandon all worldly pleasures. The seeker of the material world [*dunyā*] can never become the seeker of the Lord [*Rabb*]. Every desire must be removed from the heart until it is empty, and one can say:

> *Every desire has departed from my heart,*
> [*O Allah*] *Come now* [*into my heart*], *now there is solitude.*

It is necessary to pass three stages in order to abandon everything besides Allah ﷻ.

Stage One: Estranging One's Own Existence

All the desires of the lower self [*nafs*] must be abandoned. Until the seeker [*sālik*] vanquishes his *nafs*, he will not reach his Lord.

> *In the end, I lost all awareness of my own self,*
> *When at last I was apprised of my Lord.*

Stage Two: Abandoning the Material World

The pleasures of the *dunyā* must be relinquished. Indeed, this is a difficult task.

Absorbed in the remembrance of Allah,
The heart is granted kingship,
But it is no simple feat to forsake the dunyā *and all that it contains.*

Stage Three: Diverting One's Primary Focus From the Blessings of the Ākhirah

A *sālik* should not solely seek the blessings of the Hereafter in reward for his worship [*'ibādāt*], but must also become a seeker of the True Bestower ﷻ.

An ascetic will attain his goal,
Only when he forsakes all,
Now that you have forsaken the material world,
Forsake the rewards of the Hereafter as well.

ABUNDANCE OF *TAHLĪL*

The continual reciting of "*Lā ilāha illa'Llāh*"[28] is called *tahlīl.* This is a powerful weapon; it annihilates all false deities that may reside in one's heart.

When the flame of love roars,
All besides the Beloved are extinguished,
The sword of 'Lā' *destroys all but the True One,*
See what remains thereafter,
It is Allah who remains, all else has vanished,
Welcome, O love, a warm welcome to you.

REFLECTION [*FIKR*]

Reflection is essential in attaining love for Allah ﷻ. In this method of *dhikr*, a *sālik* imagines that the spiritual blessings [*faidh*] of Allah ﷻ are descending on his heart. He should keep in mind the following two hadiths:

---

[28] *Lā ilāha illa'Llāh* literally means, "There is no god except Allah."

إنما الأعمال بالنيات

Verily, actions are based upon intentions.

and,

أنا عند ظن عبدي بي

I (Allah) am to My servant as he thinks of Me.

The greatest amount of spiritual blessing [*faidh*] is obtained through reflection [*fikr*]. *Fikr* is the method of *dhikr* practiced from the tenth to the final lesson of the Naqshbandi *tarīqah* [spiritual path].[29]

My heart yearns for those unfilled days and nights,
When I would remain in reflection, thinking of my Lord.

COMPANY OF THOSE WHO ARE TRUE IN WORD AND DEED [*SĀDIQĪN*]

Allah ﷻ states:

يأيها الذين آمنوا اتقوا الله و كونوا مع الصادقين

O you who believe, fear Allah, and be with the truthful ones. (9:119)

If a *sālik* keeps the company of lovers, he too will become an *'āshiq*. Giving a pledge of self-rectification [*bay'ah*] to a *shaykh* and

---

[29] There are thirty-five lessons of the Naqshbandi Mujaddidi *tarīqah*. The great scholars of our ummah derived these from principles established by the Quran and *sunnah*. From the first to the seventh lesson, the emphasis is on the *dhikr* [remembrance] of the name "Allah." The eighth and ninth lesson consist of *tahlīl* [the continual recitation of *Lā ilāha illa'Llāh*]. From the tenth lesson onwards, emphasis is placed on *fikr* [reflection], wherein a seeker contemplates upon the mercy and blessings of Allah ﷻ descending upon his heart.

spending time in a sanctuary devoted to spiritual reform [*khānaqah*] are the practical ways of keeping the company of the truthful ones [*sādiqīn*]. Once *Hadrat* Shah Fazlur Rahman Ganj Muradabadi (rah) asked *Maulānā* Muhammad Ali Moongiri (rah) if he had ever seen a store where love [*'ishq*] could be obtained. He thought for a moment and then replied, "*Hadrat*, I have seen two such shops. One, the *khānaqah* of *Hadrat* Shah Ghulam Ali Dehlawi (rah) and the other, the *khānaqah* of *Hadrat* Shah 'Afaq (rah)."[30] By spending a few days in the company [*suhbah*] of a *shaykh*, a person's heart is transformed and his entire life is changed.

> *The scenes of the Day of Judgment have been embedded in my heart,*
> *By spending but a few days under an attentive gaze.*

The *shaykh* directs the *sālik* to perform *dhikr* abundantly in the secluded confines of the *khānaqah*.

> *My* shaykh *has erased the gulf between You and me,*
> *By teaching me the essence of* 'Lā ilāha illa'Llāh.'

When a *sālik* feels the love for Allah ﷻ increase in his heart, supplications [*du'āt*] for his *shaykh* pour from his heart.

> *O Lord, let the tavern of my* shaykh *remain full of patrons,*
> *For here the drink of love is given to all who come.*

A *sālik* who spent some time with *Hadrat* Shah 'Afaq (rah) described the beneficial effects of his company in these words:

---

30 Both *Hadrat* Shah Ghulam Ali Dehlawi (rah) and *Hadrat* Shah 'Afaq (rah) were prominent *shaykh*s of the Naqshbandi *tarīqah*.

O Hadrat *Shah 'Afaq, most eloquent one,*
Tell me once again the signs of Him who has no signs,
You extinguished my knowledge of syntax, grammar, and logic,
And have inflamed the fires of love for Allah.

When the heart of the *sālik* is overwhelmed with love for Allah, then every step leads to his ultimate destination.

Filled was I with love for You, wherever I turned I found only You,
I set out on the path toward You, no direction or guide with me.

The sincere lover proceeds along the way of love simply by traveling it, without a compass or a guide. The traveler wonders not whether he will reach his destination, but focuses on his journey, as he is but a traveler.

O Allah, how does one navigate this road of love?
This path moves with the traveler.

Once you set out to traverse this way of love,
Seek only the pleasure of being on the path,
Ask not one another whether the end is near or far.

PRAYER AND RECOURSE UNTO ALLAH [*ILTIJĀ'*]

When a *sālik* has done everything in his capacity, he should pray to Allah ﷻ for His help and assistance, because ultimately it is He who leads the seeker to his destination. Allah ﷻ states:

و لولا فضل الله عليكم و رحمته ما زكى منكم من أحد أبدا و لكن الله يزكي من يشاء

Were it not for Allah's grace upon you and His mercy, not one of you would ever be purified. But, Allah purifies whom He wishes. (24:21)

The blessing of love for Allah ﷻ is rapidly acquired by rising in the last portion of the night and crying profusely while making *du'a*. The blessed Prophet ﷺ preferred the following supplications [*du'at*], as mentioned in hadiths:

اللهم اجعل حبك أحب إلي من نفسي و أهلي و من الماء البارد

O Allah, make Your love more beloved to me than my own self, my family and cold water.

اللهم اجعل حبك أحب الأشياء إلي و كلها و خشيتك أخوف الأشياء عندي و اقطع عني حاجات الدنيا بالشوق إلى لقائك و إذا اقرت أعين أهل الدنيا من دنياهم فاقرر عيني من عبادتك

O Allah, make Your love the most beloved thing to me of all loves, and make my fear of You be the most fearful thing to me of all fears. Free me from the necessities of this world, by [granting me] *a desire to meet You. When the eyes of the people of the world are cooled by their worldly belongings, let my eyes be cooled by Your worship.*

اللهم اجعلني أخشاك كأني أراك أبدا حتى ألقاك

O Allah, let me fear You as though I always see You, until I meet You.

اللهم إني أسئلك إيمانا يباشر قلبي و يقينا صادقا حتى أعلم أنه لا يصيبني إلا ما كتنت و وصنا من المعيشة بما قسمت لي

O Allah, I ask of You faith which enlightens my heart and certainty such that I know that nothing will afflict me except that which You have written, and only that livelihood will I receive which You have apportioned for me.

اللهم أني أسئلك التوفيق لمحابك من الأعمال و صدق و التوكل عليك و حس
ظن بك

O Allah, I ask of You the success to do those acts beloved to You, [*and ask of You*] *truthfulness, trust, and reliance upon You, and good thoughts about You.*

اللهم أني أسئلك نفسا بك مطمئنة تؤمن بلقائك ترضى لقضائك و تقنع بعطائك

O Allah, I ask of You a contented soul and faith in meeting with You, and contentment with Your decree, and satisfaction with that which You bestow upon me.

اللهم افتح مسامع قلبي لذكرك. أنت ترحمى فارحمني رحمة تغيني بها عن
رحمة من سواك

O Allah, open my heart to Your remembrance. You are Merciful, have mercy upon me — a mercy which will render me independent of others' mercies.

اللهم أني أسئلك قلوبا أواهة مخبتة منيبة في سبيلك

O Allah, I ask of You a heart that is humble and repentant, in Your path.

اللهم اجعل وساوس قلبي خشيتك و ذكرك و اجعل همتي و هوائي فيما
ترضى

O Allah, make the whispers of my heart [*to be*] *Your fear and Your remembrance, and make my desires and aspirations in conformity with Your pleasure.*

اللهم أقسم لنا من خشيتك ما تحول به بيننا و بين معاصينا

O Allah, decree for us Your fear, such that it will form a barrier between us and our sins.

In addition to these transmitted *du'at*, any *du'a* offered in one's own language or words, is also beneficial.

To obtain love for Allah ﷻ is no simple matter. In fact it is something that requires one's full attention and devotion.

Know that this affair of love is not an easy one,
It is a river of fire, whose depths the lover must cross.

Nevertheless, a *sālik* traverses these stations of struggle and exertion and finally prays to the Lord, Most Generous:

I wish the endless limits of Thy love,
Tis' but my naïve innocence, that I wish for such a thing.

12

THE DIFFERENCE BETWEEN A *MURĪD* AND A *MURĀD*

The travelers on the path of love are of two types. The first is called a *murīd* [seeker], and denotes one whose progress is based on his own effort and worship. The second is called a *murād* [one who is sought], and denotes a person whom the Beloved ﷻ Himself wishes to draw near to Him.

The difference between a *murīd* and a *murād* may be understood by comparing the lives of Prophet Musa ﷺ and the blessed Prophet Muhammad ﷺ. Prophet Musa ﷺ was a *lover* of Allah [*muhibbullah*], while the blessed Prophet ﷺ was the *beloved* of Allah [*mahbūbullah*]. This distinction is highlighted by the following examples:

Example Number One

Prophet Musa ﷺ was granted a meeting with Allah ﷻ at Mount Sinai. Allah ﷻ narrates:

و لما جاء موسى لميقتنا

And when Musa came to meet Us. (7:143)

However, when the blessed Prophet ﷺ was granted a meeting with Allah ﷻ during the Ascension [*mi'rāj*], Allah ﷻ stated:

سبحان الذي أسرى بعبده

Glorified is He who brought His slave for a journey at night. (17:1)

The verb "came" [*jā'a*] is used for Prophet Musa ﷺ whereas the verb "brought" [*asrā*] is used for the blessed Prophet ﷺ. Prophet Musa ﷺ was told where to *come* for the meeting, whereas the blessed Prophet ﷺ was sent an angel to *bring* him to the meeting.

The enamored one is brought by the Beloved to the gathering,
Whilst the seeker [sālik] *is shown the direction from afar.*

Example Number Two

Prophet Musa ﷺ prayed:

رب اشرح لي صدري

O my Lord, expand my breast for me. (20:25)

Whereas, regarding the blessed Prophet ﷺ, Allah ﷻ revealed:

ألم نشرح لك صدرك

Have We not expanded for you your breast? (94:1)

Example Number Three

Prophet Musa ﷺ had to climb Mount Sinai to receive revelation, whereas the Quran was sent to the blessed Prophet ﷺ:

فإنه نزله على قلبك بإذن الله

It is he (Gabriel) who has revealed (this scripture) upon your heart by Allah's leave. (2:97)

The ways of love dictate that the lover [*muhibb*] hopes and desires to meet the Beloved [*mahbub*] ﷻ. Yet sometimes the Beloved ﷻ also desires that the lover come to meet Him. And when the Beloved ﷻ also wishes to meet, then it becomes easy to draw near to Him.

When the Most Beautiful One ﷻ arranges a meeting, then the true pleasure of love [*'ishq*] is attained. When the lover knows that the Beloved ﷻ loves him as well, then his happiness knows no bounds.

The love of the lover manifests in deep sighs of longing, whereas the love of the Beloved ﷻ is subtle and hidden. The love of the lover weakens his body, while the love of the Beloved ﷻ invigorates the lover's body.

The love of the Beloved is subtle and hidden,
While the love of lovers is a noticeable wound,
The love of lovers weakens the body,
Whereas, the love of the Beloved invigorates the lover.

When Allah ﷻ bestows His grace upon a servant, He opens the way to reach Him. Then the remembrance [*dhikr*] of Allah ﷻ predominates.

The call to love was issued throughout the worlds,
Yet he whom the Beloved Himself loved,
Was granted the remembrance of the Beloved.

Understand that since the goal can be attained only with the help of Allah ﷻ, He alone should be called upon:

اللهم يا قاضي الحاجات و يا دافع البليات
و يا حل المشكلات و يا كافي المهمات
و يا شافي الأمراض و يا منزل البركات
و يا سبب الأسباب و يا رافع الدرجات و يا مجيب الدعوات
و يا أمان الخائفين و يا خير الناصرين و يا دليل المتحيرين
و يا غياث المستغيثين اغثى إلهي أنت مقصودي
و رضاك مطلوبي، تركت لك الدنيا و لآخرة أتمم علي
نعمتك و ارزقني وصولك التام، بجاه سيد المرسلين
و برحمتك يا ارحم الراحمين. آمين ثم آمين

The paper is finished, the pen is finished, and we are finished,
But, the fable of desire, is still not finished.